The Mindful Journey: A Beginner's Guide

Discovering Peace and Clarity in Everyday Life

Liam Carter

Table of Contents

INTRODUCTION

"The Mindful Journey: A Beginner's Guide: Discovering Peace and Clarity in Everyday Life." This book is designed to be your guide on the illuminating path of mindfulness. Irrespective of your experience with mindfulness, this course will provide you with the abilities and understanding required to cultivate a more serene and clear mental state.

It may be challenging to find moments of presence and quiet in today's fast-paced world. We usually have too many worries about the past or nostalgic notions about the future dominating our minds, leaving little room for the present moment. Grounding our awareness in the present moment via mindfulness practice can help us overcome this modern sickness by teaching us to live more simply and plainly.

This book is not just about theory but about practical application. It aims to walk you through the foundations of mindfulness, providing valuable exercises and techniques you can immediately apply to your daily life. You will discover how to use mindfulness in all aspects of your life, including body scan meditations, breath awareness, and mindful meals and communication.

As you embark on this journey, I hope that reading these pages will bring you a deep sense of calm and clarity that can transform your daily life. It will also teach you how to overcome typical challenges and advance your mindfulness practice. Please know that I am here to support you. Best wishes on your trip.

CHAPTER I

Get To Know Mindfulness

What is Mindfulness?

Fundamentally, mindfulness focuses on the here and now in a welcoming and nonjudgmental way. There are several ways to cultivate this mental state, but meditation is the most popular method. Although "mindfulness" has gained popularity as a buzzword in modern culture, its origins are profound and date back thousands of years. Understanding mindfulness's definition, historical background, and numerous advantages are necessary to appreciate the practice truly.

A standard definition of mindfulness is meditation, in which the practitioner concentrates on paying close attention to what they are sensing and experiencing right now, without judgment or interpretation. This entails awareness of one's breathing, physical feelings, and mental thinking. The objective is to see the present moment as it is, allowing ideas and feelings to come and go without attachment rather than empty the mind or reach a state of happiness. By promoting awareness and acceptance, this practice helps people to live life to the fullest as it happens.

Since awareness is a critical component of the road to enlightenment in Buddhist traditions, these traditions are where mindfulness has its historical roots. One of the seven components of enlightenment in Buddhism, mindfulness, or satin as it is known in Pali, the language of the earliest Buddhist teachings, is central to the Noble Eightfold Path. The Buddha imparted mindfulness as a means of developing moral character, knowledge, mental discipline, and an understanding of the nature of suffering. The Buddha describes the four pillars of mindfulness—mindfulness of the body, feelings, mind, and mental phenomena—in the Satipatthana Sutta, one of the key scriptures on mindfulness. These exercises aimed to give practitioners a better understanding of how transient and linked everything is.

Although mindfulness originated as a Buddhist practice in antiquity, it has been modified and secular. The University of Massachusetts Medical School's emeritus professor of medicine, Jon Kabat-Zinn, is largely responsible for the modern mindfulness movement. Kabat-Zinn created the Mindfulness-Based Stress Reduction (MBSR) method in the late 1970s. It combined mindfulness techniques with research from contemporary psychology and neuroscience. Since its introduction, this program—which sought to assist patients in managing stress and chronic pain—has been extensively embraced in various educational, psychological, and medical contexts.

Numerous facets of mental, emotional, and physical health have been shown to improve from mindfulness, as evidenced by multiple studies. The decrease in stress is among the main advantages. Chronic stress is a widespread problem in contemporary society that has been linked to several health issues, such as diabetes, heart disease, and mental health issues. It has been demonstrated that mindfulness techniques, such as meditation and mindful breathing, cause the body to go into relaxation mode, which lowers cortisol levels and fosters a feeling of peace and wellbeing.

Emotional regulation is also improved by mindfulness. People can enhance their mastery over their affective responses by cultivating an impartial consciousness of ideas and emotions. This improved emotional intelligence lessens the effects of unpleasant emotions like anger, anxiety, and despair by enabling healthier reactions to difficult circumstances. Research has demonstrated that mindfulness-based therapies can enhance general mood and emotional stability while also dramatically reducing symptoms of anxiety and depression.

A further noteworthy advantage of mindfulness is enhanced cognitive function and concentration. The capacity to stay focused is becoming more and more critical in a society with many distractions. Mindfulness exercises improve cognitive flexibility and attention span by teaching the mind to be present. Studies have indicated that consistent mindfulness meditation can result in anatomical modifications to the brain, such as heightened density of gray matter in areas linked to memory, learning, and emotional control.

Moreover, mindfulness encourages deeper reflection and self-awareness. People can increase their awareness of their thoughts, feelings, and physical sensations by engaging in mindful practices. Increased self-awareness can help people better understand themselves and their motivations, promoting self-compassion and personal development. Through impartial observation of one's ideas, people can spot harmful tendencies and actively work to alter them.

Beyond its beneficial effects on the individual, mindfulness meditation also positively affects interpersonal connections. Mindful people often display More empathy and compassion, which can improve relationships and communication. To build stronger connections and lessen conflict, mindful people can listen and respond more carefully when present in an engagement.

It has also been demonstrated that mindfulness enhances physical wellness. Frequent mindfulness practice has been linked to several advantages for physical health, such as lowered blood pressure, enhanced immunological response, and lessened chronic pain symptoms. A key component of general health is the mind-body link, and mindfulness exercises support mental and physical health alignment.

Mindfulness has been incorporated into curricula in educational contexts to support students with stress management, focus improvement, and emotional wellbeing. Schools that use mindfulness programs report increases in students' social skills, behavior, and academic achievement. Teachers may give kids and teenagers valuable tools to deal with the difficulties of growing up in a fast-paced, digitally linked society by teaching them mindfulness.

Mindfulness training programs have become increasingly popular in the workplace to lower stress levels, increase output, and boost job satisfaction. When businesses adopt mindfulness training, employee wellbeing generally rises while absenteeism and burnout frequently decline. It has also been demonstrated that mindful leadership, which combines mindfulness concepts with management techniques, produces more resilient and upbeat business cultures.

There are many advantages to the application of mindfulness in healthcare. Traditional medical treatments are supplemented with mindfulness-based interventions, especially for long-term ailments like pain, cancer, and cardiovascular illnesses. Patients who practice mindfulness frequently report increased quality of life, decreased side effects from therapy, and better pain control. Furthermore, mindfulness practitioners in the medical field report improved patient outcomes and reduced levels of stress and burnout.

Additionally, mindfulness has a revolutionary effect on the treatment of mental illness. Developed by Zindel Segal, Mark Williams, and John Teasdale, mindfulness-based cognitive therapy (MBCT) blends mindfulness techniques with conventional cognitive behavioral therapy. MBCT has shown especially promising in preventing depressive relapses by teaching participants new techniques for better controlling their thoughts and emotions. This strategy has added to the repertoire of mental health practitioners by providing an empirically supported way to treat a range of psychological problems.

The area of addiction therapy has acknowledged the advantages of mindfulness. Through cultivating healthy coping skills and a heightened awareness of their triggers and desires, mindfulness activities support people in recovery. In order to promote long-term sobriety and avoid relapse, programs like Mindfulness-Based Relapse Prevention (MBRP) offer systematic mindfulness training. Through cultivating an impartial consciousness of ideas and feelings, people can escape the cyclone of addiction and establish a more well-rounded and satisfying existence.

The field of sports and performance development has also embraced mindfulness. When mindfulness exercises are included in their training, athletes and performers frequently report increased attention, less anxiety, and improved performance. When practicing mindfulness, people may perform at their best without being distracted or hampered by self-doubt in high-pressure situations.

Mindfulness is also essential when it comes to creativity and invention. Mindfulness has been shown to improve problem-solving skills and stimulate creative thought by cultivating an open, nonjudgmental state of awareness.

Mindfulness practitioners frequently describe being better able to think creatively and unconventionally. This can be especially helpful in industries like science, technology, and the arts requiring creativity and adaptability.

Though it has numerous advantages, mindfulness is not a cure-all and is only sometimes appropriate for everyone. Mindfulness activities can be difficult or upsetting for some people, especially those who suffer from specific mental health issues. It's critical to approach mindfulness from a balanced stance, understanding that while it can be an effective technique for some people, it might not be the best fit for others.

Maintaining the authenticity and breadth of mindfulness practice as it continues to grow in acceptance is critical. While there are many circumstances in which mindfulness can be applied, its fundamental ideas of present-moment awareness and nonjudgmental acceptance must always be upheld. Some worry that the traditional teachings of mindfulness may be compromised due to its commercialization. Consequently, to maintain the authenticity of mindfulness and make it available to a broader audience, practitioners and instructors must work hard.

To sum up, mindfulness is a timeless discipline with significant advantages for physical, mental, and emotional health. Its characterization as a judgment-free condition of present-moment awareness offers a straightforward but effective foundation for fostering calm and clarity in day-to-day living. With its roots in historical Buddhist practices, mindfulness has been modified and made secular to fit the demands of modern culture. The advantages of mindfulness are numerous and well-backed by research, ranging from stress reduction and improved emotional control to increased focus and self-awareness. As mindfulness develops and permeates more facets of contemporary life, it can change people's lives and foster a more considerate and caring society.

The Science Behind Mindfulness

Mindfulness, the practice of cultivating present-moment awareness and non-judgmental acceptance, has garnered significant attention in recent years for its roots in ancient traditions and its scientifically validated benefits. Advances in neuroscience and psychology have provided compelling evidence that mindfulness profoundly affects the brain and overall well-being. This section delves into the science behind mindfulness, exploring how it impacts the brain and highlighting critical research studies that support its effectiveness.

Mindfulness practice involves focusing on the present moment, often through meditation, and observing thoughts, feelings, and sensations without judgment. This seemingly simple practice has been shown to bring about structural and functional changes in the brain. One of the primary areas affected by mindfulness is the prefrontal cortex, the part of the brain responsible for higher-order cognitive functions such as decision-making, attention, and self-regulation. Studies have demonstrated that mindfulness meditation increases the thickness of the prefrontal cortex, indicating enhanced neural connectivity and improved cognitive functioning.

The amygdala, a region of the brain associated with emotional regulation and the stress response, is also significantly influenced by mindfulness practice. The amygdala is often referred to as the brain's "fear center" because it plays a crucial role in processing emotions such as fear and anxiety. Research has shown that mindfulness can reduce the activity and volume of the amygdala, leading to decreased emotional reactivity and a more balanced stress response. This neural adaptation helps individuals manage stress more effectively and maintain emotional stability.

The hippocampus, a critical region for memory formation and learning, also benefits from mindfulness. Mindfulness meditation has been associated with increased gray matter density in the hippocampus, suggesting that it can enhance memory retention and cognitive flexibility. These changes are particularly relevant in the context of aging, as they may help mitigate cognitive decline and improve overall brain health.

Functional MRI (fMRI) studies have provided further insights into how mindfulness affects brain activity. One of the key findings is the enhanced connectivity between the prefrontal cortex and the default mode network (DMN). The DMN is a network of brain regions active when the mind is at rest and not focused on the external environment. It is often linked to mind-wandering and self-referential thoughts. Mindfulness practice has decreased DMN activity, reducing the tendency for rumination and self-criticism. This shift in brain activity helps individuals stay more present and engaged in their current experiences.

In addition to these structural and functional changes, mindfulness also affects neurotransmitter systems in the brain. Neurotransmitters are chemical messengers that transmit signals between neurons, influencing mood, cognition, and behavior. One of the critical neurotransmitters affected by mindfulness is serotonin, which plays a crucial role in mood regulation. Studies have shown that mindfulness practice can increase serotonin levels, contributing to improved mood and reduced symptoms of depression.

Another vital neurotransmitter influenced by mindfulness is dopamine, which is associated with reward, motivation, and pleasure. Mindfulness practice has been found to increase dopamine levels, enhancing feelings of well-being and motivation. This neurochemical change can help individuals maintain a consistent mindfulness practice and experience greater satisfaction in their daily lives.

The impact of mindfulness on the brain's neural circuits is also evident in the context of pain perception. Chronic pain is a complex condition that involves both physical and psychological components. Mindfulness-based interventions, such as Mindfulness-Based Stress Reduction (MBSR), have been shown to reduce pain perception and improve pain management. Neuroimaging studies have revealed that mindfulness can alter the brain's pain-processing pathways, leading to decreased pain sensitivity and a more adaptive response to pain.

One of the most compelling aspects of mindfulness is its ability to enhance overall brain plasticity, the brain's capacity to reorganize itself by forming new neural connections. Neuroplasticity is crucial for learning, memory, and recovery from brain injuries. Mindfulness practice promotes neuroplasticity by encouraging the growth of new neurons and strengthening existing neural connections. This enhanced brain plasticity supports cognitive flexibility, emotional regulation, and resilience in adversity.

The scientific evidence supporting the benefits of mindfulness is robust and continues to grow. Numerous research studies have investigated the effects of mindfulness on various aspects of mental and physical health. One of the pioneering studies in this field was conducted by Jon Kabat-Zinn, who developed the MBSR program. In a landmark study published in 1992, Kabat-Zinn and his colleagues demonstrated that MBSR significantly reduced chronic pain symptoms in patients with diverse medical conditions. This study paved the way for further research into the therapeutic applications of mindfulness.

In the realm of mental health, mindfulness has been extensively studied as an intervention for anxiety and depression. A meta-analysis conducted by Hofmann et al. in 2010 reviewed 39 studies on mindfulness-based interventions and found significant reductions in anxiety and depression symptoms across various populations. The study concluded that mindfulness-based interventions are effective in alleviating symptoms of anxiety and depression, making them a valuable addition to traditional therapeutic approaches.

Mindfulness has also been shown to enhance overall well-being and life satisfaction. A study conducted by Brown and Ryan in 2003 investigated the relationship between mindfulness and psychological well-being in a large sample of individuals. The researchers found that higher levels of mindfulness were associated with greater life satisfaction, emotional stability, and self-compassion. These findings highlight the potential of mindfulness to promote a sense of well-being and fulfillment in daily life.

In the context of stress reduction, mindfulness has demonstrated significant benefits. A study by David Creswell and colleagues 2014 examined the effects of an eight-week MBSR program on individuals experiencing high-stress levels. The results showed that participants who completed the MBSR program had reduced levels of perceived stress and improved markers of immune function compared to the control group. This study underscores the potential of mindfulness to enhance resilience and promote better health outcomes in the face of stress.

The impact of mindfulness on attention and cognitive function has also been a focus of scientific inquiry. A study by Zeidan et al. in 2010 investigated the effects of brief mindfulness meditation training on attention and working memory. The researchers found that four days of mindfulness meditation significantly improved participants' attention span and working memory capacity. These findings suggest that even short-term mindfulness practice can have immediate cognitive benefits.

Mindfulness has been integrated into curricula in educational settings to enhance students' academic performance and emotional well-being. A study conducted by Flook et al. in 2010 examined the effects of a mindfulness-based program on elementary school students. The researchers found that students who participated in the program improved attention, social skills, and academic performance compared to the control group. These findings highlight the potential of mindfulness to support children's development and learning.

Mindfulness has also been investigated as a tool for enhancing creativity and problem-solving abilities. A study by Colzato et al. in 2012 explored the effects of mindfulness meditation on creative thinking. The researchers found that individuals who engaged in mindfulness meditation demonstrated greater cognitive flexibility and improved performance on creative tasks. These findings suggest that mindfulness can foster a mindset conducive to innovative thinking and problem-solving.

In healthcare, mindfulness-based interventions have been integrated into treatment protocols for various medical conditions. A study by Ludwig and Kabat-Zinn (2008) reviewed mindfulness's applications in medicine. It concluded that mindfulness-based interventions are effective in managing chronic pain, cardiovascular disease, and other health conditions. The study emphasized the importance of incorporating mindfulness into integrative healthcare approaches to improve patient outcomes.

Mindfulness has also been shown to benefit healthcare providers themselves. A study by Krasner et al. 2009 investigated the effects of a mindfulness-based program on physicians. The researchers found that physicians who participated in the program reported reduced burnout, improved emotional regulation, and enhanced patient care. These findings highlight the potential of mindfulness to support the well-being of healthcare providers and improve the quality of care they deliver.

The impact of mindfulness on the brain and overall well-being is further supported by research on its effects on aging. Gard et al. 2014 examined the relationship between mindfulness practice and brain aging. The researchers found that long-term mindfulness practitioners had greater gray matter volume in regions of the brain associated with cognitive function and emotional regulation compared to non-practitioners. These findings suggest that mindfulness may help preserve brain health and mental function as individuals age.

Mindfulness has also been explored as an intervention for substance use disorders. A study by Bowen et al. in 2014 investigated the effects of Mindfulness-Based Relapse Prevention (MBRP) on individuals in recovery from substance use disorders. The researchers found that participants who completed the MBRP program had lower relapse rates and improved psychological well-being than the control group. These findings suggest that mindfulness can be an effective tool for supporting long-term recovery from addiction.

In conclusion, the science behind mindfulness reveals its profound impact on the brain and overall well-being. Through structural and functional changes in the brain, mindfulness enhances cognitive function, emotional regulation, and stress management. Research studies have consistently demonstrated the benefits of mindfulness across various aspects of mental and physical health, supporting its integration into therapeutic, educational, and healthcare settings. As our understanding of mindfulness continues to evolve, it promises to transform individual lives and contribute to a more resilient and compassionate society.

Common Misconceptions

Over the past few decades, mindfulness—the practice of keeping a moment-by-moment awareness of one's thoughts, feelings, physical sensations, and the environment—has been increasingly popular. Though mindfulness is becoming increasingly recognized and used, there are still some myths and misconceptions about it. These misconceptions may prevent people from understanding mindfulness and from using it to its full potential. The purpose of this section is to dispel these myths and provide context for the subject of mindfulness.

A common misunderstanding regarding mindfulness is that it is the same as unwinding or reaching a state of tranquility. Although mindfulness can provide calm and relaxation, awareness is the main objective of mindfulness, not relaxation. Being mindful entails examining one's thoughts and emotions, whether neutral, pleasant, or bad, without judgment. By increasing their awareness of their automatic responses and reactions, people can approach their experiences more clearly and comprehensively as they engage in this exercise. Although mindfulness can occasionally be challenging, particularly when facing unpleasant feelings or ideas, this is a typical and crucial aspect.

Another widespread misconception is that practicing mindfulness necessitates clearing one's thoughts or ceasing to think. Many believe a thought-free, blank mind is necessary for a successful mindfulness practice.

Practicing mindfulness is paying attention to thoughts that come to you without letting them consume you. The mind wanders frequently, and one of the critical components of mindfulness is learning to recognize this wandering. By gently bringing the mind back to the present moment whenever it wanders, practitioners develop the ability to maintain continuous mindfulness and focus.

Another myth is that mindfulness is exclusive to spiritual or religious individuals. Although mindfulness originated in Buddhist meditation techniques, it has been modified and made secular in various modern settings. People of different backgrounds can benefit from mindfulness techniques regardless of their religious or spiritual beliefs. Numerous secular mindfulness programs have been established to make mindfulness approachable to a broader audience without any religious overtones, including Mindfulness-Based Stress Reduction (MBSR) and Mindfulness-Based Cognitive Therapy (MBCT).

Another misconception regarding mindfulness is that it is limited to meditation. Although sitting meditation is a popular and valuable technique for developing mindfulness, it is not the only one. There are several ways to practice mindfulness, such as mindful eating, mindful listening, and walking meditation. Bringing deliberate awareness to any activity one is involved in, be it daily activities or formal meditation, is the essence of mindfulness. Thanks to this flexibility, people can apply mindfulness in ways that best fit their interests and lifestyles,

The idea that mindfulness is a panacea, or a fast treatment is another common fallacy. Some people think that by engaging in mindfulness practices, they may cure all of their problems or get rid of tension and bad feelings. Although mindfulness has many advantages, such as lower stress and better emotional control, it is not a panacea. Being mindful is a skill that takes time and patience to master. The advantages of mindfulness frequently build up over time, and rather than being a magic bullet, it can be an effective tool for coping with life's obstacles.

Another misconception is that mindfulness is simple and may be achieved quickly. In actuality, practicing mindfulness can be difficult, particularly for newcomers. It necessitates a dedication to consistently returning attention to the here and now despite difficulties or discomfort. During practice, many people discover that their thoughts wander frequently or that they get irritated or agitated. These difficulties are typical and a necessary component of learning. People who practice mindfulness regularly can become more adept at it and more at peace with it.

Another widespread misunderstanding about mindfulness is that it's a solitary activity that keeps people apart from one another. Although practicing mindfulness frequently entails time spent alone and reflecting, it can also improve relationships with others. People can become more present, empathic, and compassionate in their relationships with others by increasing their self-awareness and emotional regulation. Practices like loving-kindness meditation, which mainly encourages positive attitudes towards oneself and others, are standard in mindfulness programs. These practices foster a sense of community and connection.

The idea that mindfulness is exclusively appropriate for those with plenty of spare time or who are already mentally well is a huge fallacy. In actuality, people with a variety of difficulties, including mental health conditions like stress, anxiety, and depression, can benefit from practicing mindfulness. Studies have demonstrated the efficaciousness of mindfulness-based therapies in mitigating symptoms of several mental health disorders and enhancing general well-being. Furthermore, practicing mindfulness doesn't need a lot of time. Practicing mindfulness for a short while—a few minutes each day, for example—can significantly impact. It's consistency, not duration, that matters.

Another myth about mindfulness is that it entails doing nothing but accepting everything. Practicing mindfulness entails being unresponsive to one's environment or passive. But mindfulness calls for striking a balance between acceptance and action. Instead of responding hastily, it encourages people to watch their experiences objectively and then consider their responses. This thoughtful reaction may result in more deliberate and successful behaviors. People can gain more insight and clarity by practicing mindfulness, enabling them to make wiser decisions and lead more meaningful lives.

Another misconception is that being aware and ambitious or goal-oriented are mutually exclusive. Some individuals fear that mindfulness may sap their motivation or cause them to become less goal-focused. On the other hand, by enhancing focus, resilience, and emotional regulation, mindfulness can improve the achievement of goals. When present and attentive, people can approach their goals with greater clarity and determination. In the long run, mindfulness can help people maintain their enthusiasm and endurance by assisting them in managing obstacles and disappointments more skillfully.

Another myth is that children should not practice mindfulness; it is only suitable for adults. Children can benefit significantly from mindfulness, and it has been demonstrated that mindfulness can also help young individuals. Age-appropriate mindfulness exercises for kids generally include body scans, mindful play, and mindful breathing. According to research, children who practice mindfulness can enhance their social skills, emotional control, and attention span. Education institutions and instructors are progressively integrating mindfulness programs into their curricula to improve their students' mental and emotional health.

The idea that mindfulness is an escape or avoidance strategy is prevalent. Some people think practicing mindfulness is escaping reality or avoiding uncomfortable feelings and circumstances. But mindfulness is about accepting and being more aware of reality. It entails being aware of and mindful of one's experiences, emotions, and thoughts without attempting to ignore or repress them. Instead of avoiding obstacles, people can face challenges and difficulties with more resilience and clarity when they cultivate a mindful awareness.

Another myth is that problem-solving or critical thinking cannot coexist with mindfulness. Some individuals are concerned that practicing mindfulness could impair their critical thinking ability or make them less analytical. Cognitive skills like problem-solving, concentration, and memory can all be improved by mindfulness. Mindfulness can facilitate more productive and innovative thinking by helping to maintain a clear and focused mental space. People can approach issues with a clear head and less prejudice, which improves decision-making and lessens cognitive bias.

Another fallacy is that mindfulness is a fad or trend. Although it has become more popular recently, mindfulness is not a fad. Its origins date back thousands of years, and a sizable body of scientific research attests to its advantages. The beneficial impacts of mindfulness on mental, emotional, and physical health have been shown in several research. The increasing popularity of mindfulness reflects people's understanding of its benefits and applicability in dealing with today's problems, including stress, mental health problems, and the pressures of modern living.

Lastly, there must be a misperception that practicing mindfulness necessitates rigorous practices or a significant lifestyle change. Some individuals think engaging in mindfulness entails changing one's lifestyle or adhering to strict schedules. Mindfulness is adaptable and can be incorporated into daily routines to suit timetables and personal preferences. People can apply mindfulness in meaningful and valuable ways to their daily lives, whether through formal meditation practices or informal mindfulness exercises.

In summary, mindfulness is a valuable technique with a long history and a substantial body of research to back it up. Still, many false beliefs and misconceptions regarding mindfulness prevent individuals from comprehending it entirely and using it to its full potential. Mindfulness is about developing present-moment awareness and nonjudgmental acceptance, not only about unwinding or reaching a blank mind. It only works for those who identify as spiritual or religious; it only needs a little time or significant lifestyle adjustments. People of various ages and backgrounds, especially those dealing with mental health issues, can benefit from mindfulness. It supports a more deliberate and attentive style of living by improving cognitive abilities, emotional control, and interpersonal interactions. Individuals can better understand the benefits of mindfulness and apply it to their lives to improve their general well-being and quality of life by dispelling common misconceptions about it.

Setting Intentions for Your Mindful Journey

Starting a mindful journey can be a life-changing experience to improve your general well-being, encourage emotional equilibrium, and develop a closer relationship with the outside world and yourself. Setting intentions is one of the fundamental techniques that can facilitate and enhance this journey. Intentions are guiding principles that center on the present and align with your underlying beliefs and wants, as opposed to goals, which are frequently outcome-oriented. This section explains how important it is to create intentions for your mindful journey and provides helpful advice on how to do so.

Setting intentions is a potent technique for developing mindfulness and purpose in daily life. By keeping you anchored in the here and now and constantly reminding you of what is really important, intentions provide you with a sense of purpose and clarity. As opposed to goals, which are particular accomplishments you hope to accomplish in the future, intentions are about who you want to be and what you want to live every minute of your life. For instance, one could set out to approach every day with patience, thankfulness, or compassion. This change in emphasis from result to process fosters the development of a mindful mindset transferable to all facets of life.

Developing self-awareness and self-reflection is one of the main advantages of creating aims. Setting intentions involves pausing, thinking about your goals and values, and stating what you want to develop. Mindful living requires a greater awareness of oneself and one's motivations, which is fostered by this reflection. You can cultivate a practice of self-inquiry that can uncover unconscious or automatic thought and behavior patterns by regularly creating and reviewing your aims. You can make more deliberate decisions consistent with your goals and values because of your increased self-awareness.

Setting intentions is also essential for developing resilience and a positive outlook. Setting an intention is a deliberate decision to direct your attention toward virtues like acceptance, kindness, and patience. By focusing on this, you can develop a constructive internal dialogue and divert your attention from self-deprecating or opposing ideas. By constantly bringing your behaviors to your intentions, you build resilience and inner strength that will help you overcome obstacles and failures. When things get tough, you can use your intentions as a touchstone to help you remember your basic principles and find your equilibrium and center of attention.

Setting intentions can also help you feel more connected and purposeful. Aspirations and innermost values are typically reflected in intentions, intrinsically linked to a larger sense of meaning and purpose. To nurture compassion, for example, could be motivated by a desire to improve other people's lives and make the world more compassionate. You can create a sense of fulfillment and purpose that transcends individual accomplishments by directing your actions by these aims. Throughout your mindful journey, this feeling of being a part of something bigger than yourself can be a vital source of inspiration and motivation.

An essential component of mindfulness is the idea of nonjudgmental awareness, which is strongly related to establishing intentions. Setting an intention is a judgment-free way to acknowledge your goals and where you are. By fostering an atmosphere of acceptance and compassion, this nonjudgmental awareness enables you to accept your experiences for what they are and gently direct yourself toward your goals. This method differs from goal-setting, which occasionally results in pressure to meet predetermined goals and self-criticism. On the other hand, intentions stress the becoming process and promote empathy for yourself and your trip.

It would help if you took a few practical measures to make intentions for your mindful journey that work. Establish a calm and contemplative location so that you may first connect with your inner wisdom and yourself. This space might be an actual place, like a meditation nook, or it can be an imaginary place conjured up by mindfulness exercises like body scans or deep breathing. Setting meaningful and genuine aspirations requires focusing on yourself and connecting with your inner experience.

Next, reflect on yourself to determine your main goals and values. Consider the following questions: What traits do I wish to develop? Which principles are most significant to me? How do I want to be perceived by others? You can learn more about the underlying motives behind your choices and actions by considering these questions. Writing down your ideas and intentions helps them become more apparent; thus, keeping a notebook is beneficial.

Once your goals and values have been determined, state your plans in plain, upbeat terms. Make comments in the present tense that express your desires for your actions and persona. For instance, affirm your desire by saying, "I intend to approach challenges with calm and equanimity," rather than "not be stressed." Using upbeat language in the present tense strengthens your will to live out your aims in the here and now and helps establish a sense of immediacy.

Once your intentions are established, incorporate them into your routine by engaging in rituals and mindful activities. Remind yourself of your goals when you start your day by thinking back on your aims. Take daily breaks to breathe, reflect, and realign with your aims. This can be as easy as silently repeating your intention to yourself, breathing deeply a few times before beginning an activity, or adding your aim into your meditation routine. Returning to your intentions regularly can help them become more ingrained in your everyday life.

Setting intentions requires being open-minded and flexible in your approach. Because life is dynamic, as you develop and change, your intentions may also change. Review and edit frequently to ensure your intentions stay true to your values and goals. Your intentions can remain essential and relevant through this ongoing reflection and revision process, which supports your mindful journey in a genuine and experience-based manner.

Sharing your intentions with others can be a potent approach to strengthen your commitment and foster a sense of community, in addition to introspection. Think about telling a family member, close friend, or member of a mindfulness group about your aspirations. Sharing can establish stronger connections with people with similar beliefs and goals and a sense of accountability and support. Participating in a group that endorses your mindful path can offer motivation, inspiration, and a feeling of acceptance.

Developing a kind and nonjudgmental mindset toward oneself is crucial to intention-setting. It's normal to occasionally fall short of your goals or find it difficult to live them out regularly. When this occurs, acknowledge that intention-setting is a practice rather than a perfectionism and treat yourself with compassion and understanding. Reflect on any challenges or problems you face and how you can grow from them and modify your strategy. Compassionate thinking builds resilience and self-acceptance while supporting you in staying true to your goals.

Including intention-setting in your mindful journey can improve your mindfulness practice. With intentions, you may manage life's complexity with more purpose and clarity by using them as a guiding light that illuminates your route. They provide a sense of purpose and direction by constantly reminding you of your fundamental beliefs and goals. Your life will be enhanced, and your wellbeing will be supported when your actions align with your aims. This is achieved through practicing mindfulness.

In addition, establishing intentions can have a cascading influence on several facets of your life outside of your mindfulness practice. Your relationships, career, and everyday activities benefit when you consciously choose and live out your aims. Your objectives drive how you engage with people, enabling you to speak kindly and empathically. They impact how you face obstacles, empowering you to react composedly and resiliently. They help to form your daily routines by motivating you to partake in activities that promote your well-being and are consistent with your ideals.

In summary, establishing intentions is a fundamental activity for your mindful journey that develops a positive outlook, strengthens your self-awareness, and gives your life meaning and purpose. Your underlying values and goals align with your intentions and guiding principles, keeping your attention in the here and now. They give you focus and direction, bringing you back to the present and reminding you of the things that count. You can develop a mindful mindset that improves your general wellbeing and enhances your life by making intentions and living them out.

Setting intentions successfully requires the following steps: clearing a space for thought, doing self-reflection, expressing your goals in plain, upbeat language, and incorporating them into your daily routine through rituals and mindful practices. Make sure your intentions align with your beliefs and goals by revisiting and modifying them regularly—approach intention-setting with flexibility and openness. By sharing your objectives with others, you can foster a feeling of support, community, and compassion for yourself, understanding that intention-setting is a process rather than a perfect art.

You may create a guiding light that illuminates your way and gives you greater clarity and purpose when you integrate intention-setting into your mindful journey. In trying times, you can refer to your intentions as a touchstone that can reassure you of your essential principles and help you find equilibrium and centering again. They have a beneficial effect on your relationships, job, and everyday activities, among other parts of your life, outside of your mindfulness practice.

In the end, intention-setting is a potent technique that strengthens your general mindfulness and aids in your quest for more contentment and wellbeing. It supports the development of a purposeful, meaningful, and connected attitude consistent with your beliefs and goals. You may build a conscious life that embodies your highest ideals and promotes your general wellbeing by resolutely establishing and carrying out your aims.

CHAPTER II

The Foundations of Mindfulness Practice

Breath Awareness

Breath awareness is a fundamental aspect of mindfulness practice, rooted in ancient meditation traditions and validated by modern science for its numerous benefits. The power of the breath lies in its ability to anchor us in the present moment, regulate the nervous system, and foster a deep sense of inner calm and clarity. This section explores the significance of breath awareness, its science, and various techniques for cultivating mindful breathing.

The breath is a powerful and accessible tool for mindfulness because it is always with us and constantly changing. By bringing awareness to the breath, we can develop a steady and focused mind capable of observing thoughts, emotions, and sensations without becoming entangled. This practice of breath awareness cultivates a sense of inner peace and stability, which can be particularly valuable in navigating the stresses and challenges of daily life.

One of the primary benefits of breath awareness is its ability to ground us in the present moment. The breath is always happening in the here and now, and by focusing on it, we can draw our attention away from ruminations about the past or worries about the future. This shift of attention helps to quiet the mind and create a sense of spaciousness and presence. In this state of mindful awareness, we can better respond to situations with clarity and wisdom rather than reacting impulsively.

Breath awareness also plays a crucial role in regulating the nervous system. When stressed or anxious, our breath tends to become shallow and rapid, activating the sympathetic nervous system and triggering the body's fight-or-flight response. Conversely, slow and deep breathing activates the parasympathetic nervous system, promoting relaxation and safety. By consciously slowing down and deepening our breathing, we can shift our nervous system from a state of arousal to calm, reducing stress and promoting overall well-being.

Breath awareness has been shown to have numerous physiological and psychological benefits. Research indicates mindful breathing can lower blood pressure, reduce heart rate, and improve cardiovascular health. It can also enhance immune function, reduce inflammation, and promote better digestion. On a psychological level, breath awareness can alleviate symptoms of anxiety and depression, improve emotional regulation, and enhance overall mental clarity and focus.

One of the most well-known techniques for cultivating breath awareness is mindful breathing. This practice involves paying attention to the natural rhythm of the breath without trying to change it. Find a comfortable seated position and close your eyes. Begin by observing the breath flowing in and out of the body. Notice the sensations of the breath entering and leaving the nostrils, the chest's rise and fall, and the abdomen's expansion and contraction. When the mind wanders, gently bring your attention back to the breath, using it as an anchor to the present moment.

Another effective technique for breath awareness is diaphragmatic breathing, also known as belly breathing. This practice emphasizes breathing deeply into the diaphragm, the muscle located just below the lungs, rather than shallowly into the chest. To practice diaphragmatic breathing, place one hand on your chest and the other on your abdomen. As you inhale, focus on expanding your abdomen, allowing it to rise as the diaphragm contracts. As you exhale, let the abdomen fall as the diaphragm relaxes. This technique can help to deepen the breath, promote relaxation, and improve oxygen exchange in the lungs.

Box breathing, also known as square breathing, is another powerful technique for breath awareness. This practice involves inhaling, holding the breath, exhaling, and holding the breath again, each for an equal count of four. To practice box breathing, sit comfortably and close your eyes. Inhale deeply through your nose for a count of four, hold the breath for a count of four, exhale slowly through your mouth for a count of four, and hold the breath again for a count of four. Repeat this cycle several times, making the breath steady and rhythmic. Box breathing can help to calm the mind, reduce stress, and enhance focus and concentration.

Alternate nostril breathing, or Nadi Shodhana, is a traditional yogic practice that balances energy flow in the body and promotes mental clarity. To practice alternate nostril breathing, sit comfortably and use your right thumb to close your right nostril. Inhale deeply through your left nostril, then use your right ring finger to close your left nostril as you release your right nostril and exhale through the right. Inhale through the right nostril, then close it with your thumb as you release the left nostril and exhale through the left. Continue this pattern for several rounds, focusing on the smooth and even flow of breath through each nostril. Alternate nostril breathing can help to balance the nervous system, improve respiratory function, and enhance mental clarity.

The 4-7-8 breathing technique, developed by Dr. Andrew Weil, is another effective practice for breath awareness. This technique involves inhaling for a count of four, holding the breath for seven, and exhaling for a count of eight. To practice the 4-7-8 technique, sit comfortably and close your eyes. Inhale deeply through your nose for a count of four, hold your breath for seven, and exhale slowly and completely through your mouth for eight. Repeat this cycle several times, allowing the breath to become slow and steady. The 4-7-8 technique can help to reduce anxiety, promote relaxation, and improve sleep quality.

Breath counting is another simple and effective technique for cultivating breath awareness. This practice involves counting each breath cycle to help maintain focus and concentration. Sit comfortably and close your eyes. Begin by taking a deep breath in and a slow breath out. As you exhale, silently count "one." Inhale and exhale again, counting "two" on the next exhale. Continue counting each breath cycle up to ten, then start over at one. If the mind wanders or you lose track of the count, gently bring your attention back to the breath and start again at one. Breath counting can help to improve focus, enhance concentration, and promote a sense of calm and relaxation.

Loving-kindness meditation, also known as Metta meditation, is a practice that combines breath awareness with the cultivation of positive emotions. This practice involves silently repeating phrases of loving-kindness and compassion while focusing on the breath. Sit comfortably and close your eyes. Begin by bringing awareness to your breath, allowing it to become slow and steady. As you inhale, silently repeat, "May I be happy." As you exhale, repeat, "May I be healthy." Continue with additional words such as "May I be safe" and "May I live with ease." After a few minutes, expand the practice to include others, silently repeating phrases of loving-kindness for friends, family, and even those with whom you have difficulty. Loving-kindness meditation can help to cultivate positive emotions, enhance compassion, and promote a sense of interconnectedness.

Visualization is another technique that can enhance breath awareness and promote relaxation. This practice involves using the breath to guide and focus mental imagery. Sit comfortably and close your eyes. Begin by bringing awareness to your breath, allowing it to become slow and steady. As you inhale, imagine breathing in a sense of calm and relaxation. Visualize the breath as a warm, soothing light that fills your body with each inhale. As you exhale, imagine releasing any tension or stress, allowing it to dissolve and flow with the breath. Continue this visualization for several minutes, focusing on the sensations of the breath and the imagery of relaxation. Visualization can help to deepen relaxation, reduce stress, and enhance overall well-being.

The practice of mindful walking combines breath awareness with the simple act of walking. This technique involves paying attention to the sensations of the breath and the body's movement as you walk. Find a quiet place where you can stroll and undisturbed. Begin by bringing awareness to your breath, allowing it to become slow and steady. As you walk, coordinate your breath with your steps, inhaling for a few steps and exhaling for a few steps. Focus on the sensations of the breath and the movement of your feet, legs, and body. Mindful walking can help to integrate breath awareness into daily activities, promote relaxation, and enhance mindfulness.

In addition to these techniques, incorporating breath awareness into daily routines can enhance mindfulness and well-being. Begin and end your day with a few minutes of mindful breathing, using it to set the tone for the day ahead or unwind before sleep. Practice conscious breathing during moments of transition, such as before starting a task, during a break, or while waiting. Use breath awareness as a tool for grounding and centering during stressful or challenging situations. Integrating breath awareness into daily life allows you to cultivate a continuous and mindful presence that supports overall well-being.

Breath awareness is a powerful and accessible practice that can enhance mindfulness, reduce stress, and promote well-being. The power of the breath lies in its ability to anchor us in the present moment, regulate the nervous system, and foster a deep sense of inner calm and clarity. By cultivating breath awareness through various techniques such as mindful breathing, diaphragmatic breathing, box breathing, alternate nostril breathing, the 4-7-8 technique, breath counting, loving-kindness meditation, visualization, and mindful walking, we can harness the transformative potential of the breath to enhance our lives.

Ultimately, breath awareness is about developing a deeper connection with us and the present moment. It invites us to pause, breathe, and be, allowing us to experience the richness and fullness of each moment. Through consistent practice, breath awareness can become a cornerstone of our mindfulness journey, supporting us in navigating the complexities of life with greater ease, clarity, and compassion. Whether new to mindfulness or seasoned practitioners, the breath is a powerful ally that can guide us toward greater well-being and inner peace.

Body Scan Meditation

A potent mindfulness technique called body scan meditation focuses on the physical sensations in various body areas. This meditation helps practitioners relieve tension, lower stress levels, and improve their general well-being by cultivating awareness and connection to the body. Body scan meditation promotes relaxation and mindfulness by focusing on different body areas. It also facilitates a non-judgmental study of bodily sensations. This section explores the theory behind body scan meditation, its advantages, and the process of doing a guided body scan meditation.

Ancient mindfulness traditions, especially Buddhist meditation practices, are the foundation of body scan meditation. Programs for mindfulness-based stress reduction (MBSR), created by Jon Kabat-Zinn, have helped to promote it in the West. MBSR is an eight-week program designed to help people manage stress, pain, and other physical and emotional issues by including mindfulness practices such as body scan meditation. Because the body scan offers a systematic and approachable approach to developing awareness and calm, it is frequently utilized as an introductory exercise for individuals new to mindfulness.

The basic idea behind body scan meditation is to deliberately and methodically focus attention on various body areas. Through this exercise, one might become more acutely aware of bodily sensations, which are sometimes missed or disregarded in daily life. People can develop a closer relationship with their bodies and increase self-awareness by learning to tune into these feelings, which can provide them with insight into their emotional and physical states.

Reducing stress and promoting relaxation is one of the main advantages of body scan meditation. By drawing attention to tight or uncomfortable places and allowing them to soften and relax, the exercise promotes the release of physical tension. The parasympathetic nervous system, which balances the body's stress reaction and fosters peace and well-being, mediates this relaxation response. Studies have indicated that daily body scan meditation can lower blood pressure, enhance cardiovascular health, and reduce cortisol levels.

Body scan meditation offers significant psychological benefits in addition to its physical ones. Through practicing mindfulness of bodily sensations, individuals can improve their emotional control and lessen the symptoms of depression and anxiety by increasing their feeling of presence and awareness. By decreasing self-criticism and fostering a positive self-image, the practice of non-judgmental observation during a body scan assists people in becoming more accepting and sympathetic toward themselves. Learning to maintain attention on the body and gently refocus the mind when it strays is another way that practicing mindful awareness can help people become more focused and concentrated.

The first step in body scan meditation is to locate a peaceful, quiet area where you can lie down or sit without being bothered. Establishing a space free from disturbances and distractions that promotes focus and relaxation is critical. With your back straight and your body at ease, you can sit on a chair or lie on a mat. If it is more comfortable for you, close your eyes or gently focus them on something before you.

Take a few deep breaths to let your body relax, and your mind becomes clear and concentrated before starting the body scan. Release whatever tension or stress you may be carrying as you exhale, enabling yourself to present yourself in this moment fully. Focus on your feet and note any pressure, tingling, warmth, or coldness that may be felt there. For a short while, let your attention stay on your feet. Notice these feelings without passing judgment or feeling compelled to make any changes.

Component by component, slowly and deliberately bring your focus up through your body. Start at your feet and focus on your ankles, then move your awareness to your lower legs, knees, and thighs. Please take note of any feelings you may have in each location and observe them openly and curiously. As you keep looking up, focus on your hips, lower back, abdomen, and chest. When working with each body part, take your time and give yourself enough time to explore the sensations there thoroughly.

You may experience pain, stiffness, or tightness in certain places of the body as you move through it. Instead of attempting to alter or oppose these feelings, notice them with compassion and objectivity. Envision that you are illuminating every region with a caring light, allowing everything to exist just as it is. As the body and mind learn to let go of resistance and be present with what is, this acceptance can aid in releasing tension and promoting relaxation.

Attention your hands, fingers, shoulders, and arms while scanning your upper body. Take note of any pressure, tingling, warmth, or cold feelings in these places. Shift your focus to your jaw, face, neck, and throat, noting any stiffness or relaxation. Lastly, raise your consciousness to the top of your head and either notice any feelings there or relax and focus on your entire body's awareness.

After finishing the body scan, pause in this attentive awareness state for a short while, giving yourself time to experience the sensations in your body completely. Take note of your overall body sensations and any shifts in your mental or physical condition. Breathe deeply a few times and give yourself time to bring the body scan sensation into the present.

For new people, guided body scan meditations can be especially beneficial because they offer a systematic and encouraging framework for developing mindfulness. Many resources provide guided body scan meditations led by seasoned mindfulness teachers, such as audio recordings, apps, and online videos. As you progress with your practice, these guided exercises can help you better understand body scan meditation and provide direction and support.

Frequent body scan meditation has several long-term advantages for mental and physical well-being. Research has indicated that persons who consistently engage in body scan meditation have reduced levels of stress, anxiety, and sadness. They also report better general well-being, emotional stability, and sleep quality. In addition to fostering better relationships with the body and increasing body awareness, body scan meditation can help people adopt a more tolerant and loving mindset toward themselves.

Body scan meditation in your daily practice can help you develop awareness and improve your general well-being. As you grow more accustomed to the practice, progressively extend the length of your sessions from shorter ones—ten to fifteen minutes, for example. Body scan meditation can be done in the morning to help you start your day mindfully, in the evening to help you wind down before bed, or when you need a quick moment of grounding and relaxation.

Combining body scan meditation with mindfulness techniques like mindful breathing, loving-kindness meditation, or mindful movement can also be beneficial. Integrating these techniques may create a comprehensive mindfulness practice that promotes physical and mental well-being. For instance, you may start a meditation session with mindful breathing to help you center yourself. Then, you can do a body scan to increase your awareness of your physical sensations. Finally, you could finish the session with a loving-kindness meditation to help you develop compassion and happy feelings.

You can also practice body scan meditation informally by paying attention to your body while engaging in daily activities. For instance, while you're eating, walking, or sitting at your work, take a moment to check in with your body. Observe any areas that feel tense or relaxed, then gently direct your attention there with an open mind and feeling of inquiry. This unstructured exercise can support a constant level of awareness and presence and assist in incorporating mindfulness into your everyday life.

Besides its advantages, body scan meditation can be a helpful instrument in therapeutic environments. Body scan meditation is one of the mindfulness-based techniques that have been used to help people with a variety of mental and physical health issues, such as anxiety, depression, chronic pain, and post-traumatic stress disorder (PTSD). Body scan meditation can help people cultivate a more compassionate relationship with their bodies and lessen the effects of physical and emotional suffering by encouraging a non-judgmental awareness of bodily sensations.

To help patients manage their symptoms and improve their general well-being, therapists and medical professionals may use body scan meditation in therapy regimens. To help a patient learn relaxation and self-regulation techniques as well as become more conscious of the bodily signs of stress or anxiety, a therapist could lead them through a body scan meditation. As part of a more extensive self-care regimen, patients can also be encouraged to practice body scan meditation at home.

Body scan meditation is an effective and approachable mindfulness technique with many advantages for mental and physical well-being. By focusing on various bodily areas methodically, practitioners can enhance their sense of presence and connection, alleviate stress, and encourage relaxation. Body scan meditation promotes a welcoming and loving attitude toward oneself by encouraging a non-judgmental awareness of physical sensations.

For individuals who are new to the practice, guided body scan meditations can offer invaluable structure and support, which can improve knowledge and encourage regular mindfulness practice. Regular body scan meditation can provide long-term advantages such as less worry and tension, better sleep, and overall well-being. Body scan meditation can be incorporated into daily routines and combined with other mindfulness practices to help people develop a complete mindfulness practice that promotes mental and physical health.

Body scan meditation is a valuable tool for cultivating mindfulness, improving self-awareness, and fostering a sense of inner peace and well-being, whether alone or in therapeutic settings. The secret to enjoying the advantages of body scan meditation, as with any mindfulness exercise, is regular, focused practice. You can improve your general quality of life, cultivate a sense of relaxation and presence, and establish a closer relationship with your body by including body scan meditation regularly in your mindfulness practice.

Mindful Listening and Observation

Mindful listening and observing are essential elements of mindfulness practice that improve our capacity to be present and attentive in our relationships with others and our surroundings. Our relationships, communication, and general well-being can all be significantly enhanced by practicing focused observation and thoughtful listening. This section examines the ideas of attentive observation and listening and their advantages and valuable methods for developing these abilities.

The habit of entirely focusing on the speaker without interruptions or preconceived notions is known as mindful listening. It entails being present and offering the speaker our whole attention. We can fully comprehend the speaker's message, feelings, and intentions when we pay attention to this degree. Beyond just hearing what is being said, mindful listening includes observing non-verbal indicators including facial expressions, tone of voice, and body language. We may respond more carefully and sympathetically when present and paying attention, which helps build stronger bonds and more meaningful encounters.

Making the conscious decision to be present and attentive is the first step in the mindful listening process. Take some time to center yourself and eliminate any distractions from your thoughts before starting a conversation. You can achieve this by taking a few deep breaths or meditating. By consciously listening attentively, you open up a receptive mental space that facilitates complete engagement with the speaker.

Keeping an open mind and refraining from passing judgment is essential to careful listening. This entails paying attention to the speaker's words without adding your thoughts or conclusions. It involves having an open mind and being intrigued about the speaker's viewpoint, even if it differs from yours. You may foster a secure and encouraging space for the speaker to express themselves by putting your judgment aside. More open, sincere, and honest conversation is encouraged by this nonjudgmental mindset.

Active listening is a crucial component of mindful listening. To listen actively, one must comprehend the underlying motives and feelings in addition to just hearing what is being said. This necessitates closely observing the speaker's body language, facial expressions, and tone of voice. Recalling what you have listened to might also be a beneficial strategy. To ensure you have comprehended the speaker's point accurately, paraphrase or summarize what they have stated. Reflective listening demonstrates to the speaker your whole attention and appreciation for their viewpoint.

It's essential to be conscious of your inner reactions while you listen. You might become aware of your thoughts, feelings, or bodily sensations while you listen. Sometimes, these internal reactions can keep you from giving the speaker your attention. You can acknowledge these responses without allowing them to obstruct your listening ability by paying careful attention to them. Being self-aware helps you remain focused and in the moment, which makes it possible for you to listen more intently and sympathetically.

There are several advantages to mindful listening regarding personal and professional relationships. Mindful listening can promote understanding, strengthen emotional bonds, and lessen conflict in interpersonal relationships. By listening with awareness, we provide room for our loved ones to be heard and understood, which can improve our relationship. Mindful listening has been shown to boost productivity, foster better teamwork, and promote collaboration in work environments. We can improve our ability to communicate and solve problems by paying close attention to our clients' and coworkers' wants and concerns.

Another crucial component of mindfulness practice is conscious observation. It entails being observant and curious while paying great attention to our experiences and environment. By practicing mindful observation, we can pick up on subtleties and details in our experiences and surroundings that we might otherwise miss. Our everyday lives can be improved, and our appreciation of the present moment can grow due to this increased awareness.

Making the conscious decision to observe thoughtfully is the first step in the mindful observation technique. You can accomplish this by setting aside time to focus on the here and now. Take note of your environment as well as your physical experiences. Breathe deeply a few times and permit yourself to be present. By consciously establishing the goal to watch, you can open up a responsive and open mental space and interact entirely with your surroundings.

The "beginner's mind" method is one way to engage in mindful observation. This is looking at you with amazement and curiosity as if it's your first time seeing them. You can let go of assumptions and preconceptions and open yourself up to seeing things from a different perspective by taking on a beginner's mindset. By encouraging an awareness of the richness and beauty of your surroundings, this exercise can help you feel grateful and appreciative.

The practice of sensory awareness is another method of conscious observation. This entails focusing on the sights, sounds, tastes, scents, and bodily sensations that you are experiencing. You can ultimately interact and have a more vivid experience of your surroundings by raising your conscious awareness of all your senses. You can practice mindful observation, for instance, by focusing on your meal's flavor, texture, and perfume while eating. You can take in your surroundings' sights, sounds, and colors when you stroll in nature. Your overall mindfulness practice can be improved by using sensory awareness to help you remain grounded and in the moment.

Being conscious of your thoughts and feelings is another aspect of mindful observation. Observing your internal experiences with an open mind and curiosity is the practice known as mindfulness of thoughts and emotions.

You may notice your thoughts and feelings as they come and go without passing judgment or becoming attached, as opposed to becoming sucked into them. You can become more emotionally intelligent and self-aware through this exercise, improving your ability to deal with your inner experiences.

There are several advantages to practicing attentive observation for your general well-being. It can improve your sensory experiences, help you feel more present and aware, and help you connect with your surroundings on a deeper level. You can improve your ability to respond to your thoughts and emotions by practicing mindful observation, which can also help you become more self-aware and emotionally intelligent. You can develop a stronger sense of appreciation and thankfulness by interacting with your surroundings and experiences, improving your quality of life.

Developing the habit of carefully observing and listening in your daily activities can have profound effects. These abilities can strengthen your connection to the present moment, relationships, and communication. It is crucial to practice routinely and consistently to develop mindful observing and listening skills. Begin by dedicating a short period each day to the discipline of attentive observation and listening. As you get more accustomed to the techniques, gradually increase the length and frequency of your practice.

Engaging in conversations with others is a valuable technique to improve mindful listening in daily life. Decide to pay close attention to what the speaker is saying and listen with awareness. Once you've acknowledged any internal reactions, slowly return your focus to the speaker. Asking clarifying questions and thinking back on what you have heard are ways to engage in active listening. Take note of the nonverbal clues used by the speaker and reply with compassion and comprehension. You can improve communication and strengthen relationships by engaging in mindful listening during talks.

Make it your goal to observe consciously while going about your regular business if you want to integrate mindful observation into your life. For instance, while you walk, pay attention to your environment and the feelings in your body. Take note of the hues, patterns, and noises surrounding you. Consider the flavor, texture, and scent of your meal. Incorporate awe and inquiry into your sensory encounters. By being open-minded and curious while you examine your inner experiences, you can cultivate mindfulness of thoughts and emotions. You can strengthen your connection to the present moment and improve your sensory experiences by implementing mindful observation into your everyday routine.

To sum up, mindful observation and listening are crucial aspects of mindfulness practice that improve our capacity to be alert and present in our relationships with people and surroundings. To become skilled in mindful listening, one must consciously decide to stay in the moment, practice active listening, keep an open mind, and remain conscious of one's feelings. In addition to strengthening bonds between people, mindful listening can increase empathy and understanding. Setting the goal to observe, taking on a beginner's mindset, engaging in sensory awareness exercises, and being conscious of our thoughts and feelings are all components of mindful observation. Our sensory experiences can be improved, our relationship with our surroundings is strengthened, and self-awareness and emotional intelligence are developed through mindful observation. We can improve our general well-being and create a stronger feeling of presence and awareness by introducing attentive listening and observation into our daily lives. The secret to mastering these techniques and reaping the life-changing advantages of attentive observation and listening is regular, consistent practice.

Cultivating Presence

Cultivating presence and remaining in the present moment has drawn much attention lately because of its tremendous effects on general well-being, personal fulfillment, and mental health. In an environment where multitasking, constant distractions, and the fast-paced nature of contemporary life are commonplace, the capacity to stay in the present moment serves as a haven and a valuable instrument for managing everyday obstacles. Developing a conscious awareness of the now, letting go of regrets from the past and worries about the future, and ultimately embracing the experiences of the present are all part of cultivating presence. A more aware, centered, and contented life can be fostered by incorporating various presence-building techniques into many facets of one's daily routine.

Essentially, practicing presence is focusing entirely on the present moment. This entails fully bringing the senses, feelings, and ideas into the moment without diversion or criticism. The foundation of presence is awareness, which invites people to notice their thoughts and emotions without becoming attached or repulsed. A more profound appreciation of life's experiences and a stronger sense of inner peace can be attained by practicing mindfulness, which helps develop a state of consciousness in which one is present.

Mindfulness meditation is one way to cultivate the present that works best. This technique entails scheduling a regular period to sit still, concentrate on breathing, and watch the passing of ideas and sensations without becoming caught up in them. By teaching the mind to return to the moment when it wanders, mindfulness meditation strengthens mental resilience and improves the capacity to remain present all day. Regular mindfulness meditation can increase one's sense of peace, emotional stability, and clarity, making staying present during everyday tasks more straightforward.

Mindful breathing is another method for developing presence. This is observing the breath as it enters and exits the body carefully. Being present can be achieved through conscious breathing, which can be adaptable at any time or place. Through breathing exercises, people can lessen the impact of outside stimuli and distracting ideas by anchoring their consciousness in the present moment. This straightforward yet effective exercise can help you feel more at ease and in control when stressed or anxious.

Bringing awareness into daily life is another helpful strategy for developing presence. One way to achieve this is to give regular activities like eating, exercising, or even dishwashing your whole focus. For instance, when eating thoughtfully, one can concentrate on the meal's tastes, textures, and fragrances, taking their time and enjoying every mouthful. Similarly, mindful walking is awareness of the sensations derived from each step, body movement, and the surroundings. People can turn ordinary tasks into chances for mindfulness and presence by fully participating in these daily activities.

Cultivating presence in social situations also requires the skill of focused listening. This is listening intently to the speaker without stepping in or formulating a rejoinder while they are speaking. Being present with the other person while paying attention to their words, tone, and body language is necessary for mindful listening. This exercise builds empathy and deeper connections in addition to improving communication. People can respond more carefully and sincerely when they listen intently, enhancing their interactions' quality.

Practicing gratitude is another powerful way to develop the present. People can become more grounded in the here and now by taking the time each day to consider and be grateful for the good things in life rather than dwelling on their regrets and anxieties. This can be accomplished by simply taking a few minutes to appreciate the positive aspects of life in your mind or by keeping a gratitude notebook. Practicing gratitude improves general well-being and contentment by fostering a positive outlook and encouraging attention to the present.

The cultivation of the present is also supported by yoga and mindful movement techniques. By focusing on the body's alignment, sensations, and movements, these exercises help to establish a solid mental-physical bond. Engaging in mindful movement practices such as yoga relieves physical tension, heightens bodily awareness, and fosters mental serenity and clarity. These energetic and embodied mindfulness approaches benefit people who find it challenging to sit still during standard meditation sessions.

The foundation of developing presence is the idea of non-judgment. This means being aware of one's ideas and feelings without assigning them a positive or negative value. People can lessen their propensity to respond to ideas and emotions by taking a nonjudgmental stance and letting them pass without upsetting them. Through acceptance and openness, one can fully engage with the present moment without resistance or attachment, as this practice promotes. Nonjudgment creates a roomy and caring inner environment to support general mental and emotional well-being.

Including times of digital fasting in everyday life can also improve the capacity for present-moment awareness. Continuous use of social media and electronic devices can divert attention and cause people to become disengaged from the here and now. Making time each day to spend offline activities and unplug from devices makes room for presence and mindfulness. Reading a book, taking up a creative pastime, or spending time in nature are all examples of activities that offer chances to be present and savor the richness of the present moment.

Further reinforcing mindfulness and present techniques can be achieved by creating a routine. Incorporating mindfulness into daily life is simpler when you set a structured timetable for mindful movement, mindfulness meditation, and other presence-enhancing activities. Building a habit of presence requires consistency, and these activities can eventually become ingrained in a person's daily routine.

Self-compassion exercises can also help to develop mindfulness and presence. This entails showing oneself the same compassion and consideration one would provide a friend. Self-compassion creates a positive internal conversation by enabling people to accept their flaws and hardships without engaging in severe self-criticism. People can improve their general emotional resilience and well-being by developing a more compassionate and present relationship with themselves through self-compassion practices.

There are many advantages of practicing presence and being in the present moment. Individually, these techniques can result in lower stress levels, better emotional control, and a stronger sense of inner tranquility. People can escape the loop of worrying and rumination by being in the now, which leads to a better understanding of perspective and clarity. This improved mental state facilitates a deeper appreciation of life's small joys and more efficient problem-solving and decision-making.

Cultivating presence improves empathy, connection, and communication in interpersonal relationships. People can develop more profound, more genuine relationships based on respect and understanding by being present with one another. This may result in a more positive and peaceful social atmosphere and increased pleasure in personal and professional relationships.

In the workplace, being present can enhance concentration, output, and inventiveness. It can be simpler to stay involved with work and projects when mindfulness practices are used to improve attention and concentration. More concentration can result in a better job and more effective use of the available time. Furthermore, mindfulness can promote creative thinking and problem-solving, leading to success and advancement in the workplace. This is because mindfulness brings about clarity and tranquility.

Practicing presence can help create a culture that is more understanding and kind. People can make more deliberate decisions that advance their own and others' well-being as they become more conscious and present. This can promote a more optimistic and sustainable society by increasing a sense of belonging, teamwork, and shared responsibility.

To sum up, developing presence and remaining in the present are crucial skills for improving mental health, general well-being, and personal fulfillment. People can learn to be wholly present and involved in life's situations by practicing mindfulness through mindful breathing, mindful movement, mindful meditation, mindful listening, and gratitude exercises. Being present can become a regular habit by using a nonjudgmental mindset, digital detox intervals, and creating a supportive routine. Beyond the individual, developing presence positively affects relationships, career performance, and the development of a more thoughtful and compassionate community. The increasing popularity of presence as a practice can potentially change the lives of individuals and the human experience as a whole.

CHAPTER III

Mindfulness in Daily Activities

Mindful Eating

Mindful eating aims to approach food with awareness and presence, concentrating on the current moment. It entails developing a nonjudgmental attitude toward eating, focusing on food's sensory experiences, and identifying signs of hunger and fullness. The fundamentals of mindful eating strongly emphasize the role that enjoyment, intention, and mindfulness play during eating. Through mindful eating, people can strengthen their bond with their bodies, have a better relationship with food, and generally feel better about themselves. People can become more aware of their eating patterns and make more deliberate decisions about what and how they eat by engaging in various mindful eating activities and approaches.

Fundamentally, mindful eating encourages people to take their time and enjoy their food to the fullest. This is enjoying each bite of food, paying attention to its flavors, textures, and scents, and being grateful for its nutrition. Being aware of oneself is one of the cornerstones of mindful eating. This entails paying attention to the thoughts, feelings, and bodily sensations that surface when eating in the present. By increasing awareness of the eating process, people can better understand their bodies' hunger and fullness signals, making it more straightforward to determine when they are hungry and satisfied.

Another essential component of mindful eating is intention. This entails making deliberate decisions about what and how much to eat instead of eating unthinkingly or out of habit. Making conscious food choices and paying attention to portion sizes are part of intentionally eating mindfully. It also entails understanding the motivations behind eating, such as social conditions, emotional tension, or physical hunger. People can make better food decisions and have a healthier relationship with eating when they eat with intention.

Being judgment-free is a crucial component of mindful eating. This idea entails examining one's eating patterns and other activities without assigning them a positive or negative label. It involves giving up feelings of guilt, humiliation, and judgment regarding dietary decisions in favor of a kind and welcoming outlook. People can make a more supportive and upbeat environment by practicing non-judgment, lowering stress and encouraging better eating habits.

The "Raisin Exercise," frequently used in mindfulness training programs, is one of the best ways to practice mindful eating. In this practice, you will examine a raisin using all your senses. People are first asked to investigate the raisin, noting its color, shape, and texture. They are then instructed to feel the raisin, focusing on any ridges or bumps on its surface. They next inhale the aroma of the raisin by sniffing it.

At last, they put the raisin in their teeth and chew it carefully, savoring every bite and focusing on the flavors, textures, and feelings. People can practice being completely present and involved with their food by doing the raisin exercise. This practice can be extended to other meals and snacks.

One such helpful mindful eating practice is the "Mindful Meal." This practice is scheduling a time to eat without interruptions from electronics like phones, computers, or televisions. People are urged to concentrate just on eating during the mindful meal, savoring the food's flavors, textures, and scents. In addition, they are advised to pay attention to any ideas or feelings that come up, as well as their bodily cues of hunger and fullness. People who eat mindfully can become more aware of their eating patterns and make more deliberate decisions about what and how much to eat.

An additional method for engaging in mindful eating is the "Five Senses Exercise." During the eating exercise, all five senses are to be used. People are first urged to examine their food, taking note of its hues, forms, and presentation. They are then instructed to smell the dish, savoring its aroma and noting any associations or recollections that come to mind. They then make contact with the food to sense its temperature and texture. Subsequently, kids hear the noises from eating, including the crunch of vegetables or soup slurping. At last, they taste the food, enjoying every mouthful and focusing on the tastes and feelings that arise in the mouth. People can increase their awareness of and satisfaction from eating by using all five senses.

Acknowledging and respecting your body's hunger and fullness signals is another aspect of mindful eating. The "Hunger and Fullness Scale," a tool that allows people to rate their state of hunger and fullness on a scale from 1 to 10, is one way to achieve this. People are advised to assess their hunger level before consuming any food using a hunger scale, where 1 represents extreme hunger, and 10 means extreme fullness. They can periodically determine their level of fullness while eating by checking in with themselves. By doing this, people can improve their ability to recognize their body's cues and make more educated decisions about when and how much to eat.

Another crucial component of mindful eating is gratitude. Eating can be made more enjoyable, and a greater appreciation for its sustenance can be fostered by showing gratitude for the meal and the work that went into its preparation. This can be achieved by engaging in a brief, silent exercise of appreciation before eating, during which you thank and appreciate the individuals, systems, and materials that went into preparing the meal. People can connect more positively and thoughtfully with food by practicing thankfulness.

Consistency of one's emotional eating habits is another aspect of mindful eating. Many people use food as a comfort or coping mechanism for stress, boredom, or other emotions. By engaging in mindful eating practices, people can learn better coping mechanisms for their feelings and increase their awareness of the emotional triggers that lead to eating. Emotional eating can be addressed using the "Pause and Reflect" activity. This entails stopping before a meal and spending some time reflecting on oneself. People can ask themselves questions like, "Am I physically hungry?" "What emotions am I experiencing?" and "What do I need right now?" during this period of reflection. People can become more conscious of their emotional condition and make more deliberate decisions about what to eat or discover other strategies to deal with their emotions by stopping and thinking.

Mindful eating can also be supported by integrating mindfulness into the planning and preparation of meals. This is taking the time to cook meals carefully and picking foods that nourish the body. A few examples of mindful meal planning are experimenting with new recipes, choosing a range of vibrant and nutrient-dense foods, and paying attention to portion proportions. People can practice mindfulness while preparing meals by paying attention to the various sensory experiences that come with it, such as the noises of chopping vegetables, the aromas of spices, and the textures of different foods. People can create a more attentive and pleasurable dining experience by incorporating mindfulness into the planning and preparation of their meals.

To sum up, mindful eating is a technique that encourages people to be present and conscious when they eat. Consciousness, intention, and non-judgment are the guiding concepts of mindful eating, which stress the value of being in the moment, making thoughtful decisions, and developing a healthy relationship with food. People can practice mindful eating and establish a stronger connection with their body by using a variety of exercises and approaches, including the hunger and fullness scale, mindful meals, the raisin exercise, and the five senses exercise. People can develop healthier and more mindful eating habits by addressing emotional eating behaviors, recognizing and following hunger and fullness cues, and integrating mindfulness into meal planning and preparation. In addition to improving, one's pleasure in food, mindful eating improves general health and fosters a more harmonious and satisfying relationship between the body and food.

Mindful Walking

Walking while practicing mindfulness, which is the concentrated, judgment-free awareness of the present moment, is combined with the physical act of walking. This ancient practice, which originates in Buddhism and other ancient traditions, has become increasingly popular in modern wellness and mindfulness societies. To foster a closer bond between the mind and body, mindful walking entails paying great attention to the feelings, emotions, and environment encountered. Comprehending mindful walking and knowing how to do it helps improve mental, bodily, and general mindfulness.

Walking with complete awareness is the fundamental component of mindful walking. Mindful walking emphasizes the trip rather than walking as a means to an objective, like arriving at a destination. It invites people to take it slowly and pay attention to the little things—like the feel of the earth beneath their feet, the rhythm of their breathing, and the sights and sounds of their surroundings. This exercise lowers tension and fosters clarity and serenity by keeping the mind anchored in the here and now.

The foundation of mindful walking is an impartial awareness of the here and now. This entails not categorizing ideas, feelings, or experiences as they emerge as good or bad. When walking, this could entail paying attention to the sensations in the feet, how the legs move, the breathing pattern, and the different environmental cues such as sights, sounds, and scents. People can develop an awareness they can use in other aspects of their lives besides walking by concentrating on these in-the-moment experiences.

The accessibility of mindful walking is one of its main advantages. Mindful walking is a technique that may be done practically anywhere and at any time, unlike seated meditation, which calls for a quiet area and a certain amount of silence. It's a flexible and adaptive exercise that may be done indoors and outdoors in urban and natural settings. Because of its accessibility, people may include mindful walking into their regular schedules, whether taking a stroll, commuting or taking a lunch break.

Setting a clear intention at the outset is crucial to practicing mindful walking. Deciding to walk mindfully with aim aids mental concentration and directs the exercise. This goal could be as straightforward as seeking calm and relaxation or increasing awareness of the current moment. People can establish a conceptual framework to support their mindfulness practice by setting an aim.

Selecting an appropriate walking location is the first step towards mindful walking. This might be a stroll along a park path, a woodland trail, or even a section of pavement in a metropolis. Selecting a place to walk without too many interruptions or distractions is crucial. Once you've located a good spot, pause for a moment to center and center yourself. To focus on yourself, take a few deep breaths and feel the connection between your feet and the ground.

Start moving slowly and deliberately. As your feet come into contact with the ground, could you notice how they feel? Take note of the heel-to-toe gait and the weight transfer from one foot to the other. Try to time your steps to your breathing as you move. You could, for instance, walk a step for every breath in and out. The walking exercise takes on a rhythmic, contemplative quality because of this synchronization.

Bring your attention to your body as you walk. Take note of how your arms and legs move and how your body is positioned overall. Try to relax any tense or uncomfortable spots by paying attention to them. Try not to focus on anything as you take in your surroundings with a soft, unfocused gaze. This kind of look aids an open mind and an awareness of the surroundings.

Nonjudgmental awareness is a discipline that is essential to mindful walking. This entails being aware of any ideas, feelings, or experiences without categorizing them as positive or negative. For instance, acknowledge your irritation or boredom without attempting to ignore them. If your thoughts stray, gently return them to the sensations of walking and the cadence of your breathing. It is possible to develop a sense of acceptance and presence by engaging in this nonjudgmental awareness exercise.

Bringing awareness to the surroundings might be beneficial in addition to concentrating on the feelings experienced while walking. Take note of the sounds surrounding you, including the hum of traffic, the rustling of leaves, and birds chirping. Whether it is the aroma of food, flowers, or the freshness of rain, pay attention to the scents in the atmosphere. Enjoy the view while taking in the surroundings' hues, patterns, and textures. You may improve your general mindfulness practice and strengthen your connection to the present moment by using all your senses.

A crucial component of walking with mindfulness is cultivating gratitude. While strolling, savor the sensation of being able to walk and the chance to be in your preferred setting or the great outdoors. Give thanks for the air you breathe, the beauty of your environment, and your body's mobility. This thankfulness practice can improve The mindful walking experience by fostering an optimistic and appreciative mindset.

Including attentive walking as a daily habit might also be beneficial. Creating a routine of mindful walking by designating particular times of the day or week can aid in habit formation. This may be a walk in the morning to get your day started a stroll in the evening to decompress, or a mental-refreshing lunch break. By practicing mindful walking, you can develop a regular mindfulness practice that enhances your general well-being.

Walking mindfully has many advantages for the body and mind but can also strengthen one's bond with the natural world. Those who walk deliberately in natural environments can take in the peace and beauty of the surroundings. This relationship with nature can foster a greater appreciation for the environment and a sense of amazement and wonder. Additionally, it can give one a feeling of equilibrium and grounding, which can lessen tension and encourage inner serenity.

Walking mindfully can also be done in social situations, like with a group or a spouse. Walking attentively with others can improve the shared experience and feeling of connectedness. The mindfulness practice also presents a chance for encouragement and support from one another. Choosing a tempo that promotes mindfulness and establishing a collective intention can be beneficial when mindful walking with others. People can increase their sense of community and connection by sharing their experiences and observations while walking.

People can add mindful pauses to their mindful walking practice to make it even more effective. At these points in the walk, pause, take a few deep breaths, and center yourself by staying in the present. You can take a moment to reset and relax during these breaks and utilize this time to check in with your body and notice any areas of stress or discomfort. Taking deliberate breaks also lets you thank the experience and consider your intention.

Including attentive walking in other mindfulness exercises is another beneficial method. For instance, you can spend a few minutes walking mindfully to start or finish a sitting meditation session. This can facilitate the transition between various activities and help you incorporate mindfulness into your routine. Combining mindful walking with other physical activities, like yoga or tai chi, can provide a comprehensive approach to mindfulness and wellbeing.

Adapting the mindful walking technique to other settings and circumstances is also possible. You can, for instance, go indoors in a spacious room or hallway while paying attention to how it feels to walk on various surfaces. In addition, you can walk mindfully through crowded cities, paying attention to the sights, sounds, and scents of the surroundings. Create an adaptable and flexible mindfulness practice that you can incorporate into all facets of your life by situating the practice in different contexts.

To sum up, walking mindfully is a vital practice that blends mindfulness with the physical act of walking. People can develop a stronger bond between their mind and body by entirely focusing on the feelings, emotions, and environment they encounter as they walk. Walking with mindfulness cultivates awareness that may be applied to various aspects of life. These practices include nonjudgmental awareness, gratitude, and engaging with the senses. Setting goals, locating a good walking spot, paying attention to your gait, and interacting with the surroundings are all part of mindful walking. People can develop a continuous mindfulness practice that promotes general well-being by including mindful walking into their daily routine, engaging in thoughtful pauses, and customizing the practice to various contexts. Walking mindfully promotes better physical and mental health, a closer relationship with the natural world, and a stronger sense of awareness and gratitude for everyday life.

Mindful Communication

Mindful communication aims to improve understanding, lessen conflict, and forge better connections through integrating mindfulness into interpersonal communication. It entails participating in talks, listening intently, and giving intelligent, sympathetic responses. People who include mindfulness in their communication can listen intently, communicate ideas and feelings more effectively, and build deeper connections with others. Understanding mindful communication and using mindful speaking and listening techniques can significantly enhance interpersonal relationships and promote a more loving and peaceful atmosphere.

The idea of presence is the foundation of mindful communication. Being engaged in the present moment, free from distractions from the past or worries about the future, is what it means to be present. People can listen and comprehend the other person's point of view during conversations when there is a deeper level of awareness and attention due to this presence. People respond more appropriately and sincerely in conversations when fully present, which builds mutual respect and trust.

Furthermore, highlighting the value of nonjudgmental awareness is mindful communication. This means paying attention to ideas, emotions, and physical sensations as they come up during talks and not categorizing them as positive or negative. People can lessen their emotional reactions and approach communication with an open and accepting mindset by adopting a nonjudgmental attitude. This openness promotes more sincere and meaningful interactions because people feel comfortable expressing themselves without worrying about being judged or criticized.

Another essential element of attentive communication is empathy. Understanding and feeling another person's emotions is a necessary component of empathy. Through developing empathy, people can emotionally connect with others more deeply, which promotes compassion and understanding. Those who practice mindful communication are encouraged to walk in the other person's shoes and consider their experiences, feelings, and thoughts. By using empathy, we may close understanding gaps and foster a more loving and supportive atmosphere.

Mindful speaking is one of the main techniques of mindful communication. Being conscious of the words we use, the tone of our voice, and how our speech affects other people are all part of mindful speaking. It calls for speech that is purposeful, compassionate, and clear. It is crucial to pause before speaking and give our words some thought, both in terms of what we want to say and how we want to express it, to engage in mindful speaking. This break promotes introspection and can assist in avoiding rash or reactive communication.

Clear, concise, and compassionate word choice is crucial while speaking mindfully. Clear communication lowers the possibility of misconceptions by ensuring that our message is understood as intended. Concise communication respects the listener's time and attention by minimizing extraneous or repetitious material. Respect and compassion are fostered by considerate communication that takes into account the thoughts, feelings, and viewpoints of others. People can express themselves more politely and successfully with kindness, conciseness, and clarity.

Being conscious of our voice tone is another part of speaking mindfully. Many different feelings and objectives can be expressed by tone, often even more effectively than words. While a harsh or aggressive tone might incite tension and defensiveness, a pleasant and quiet tone can create a feeling of safety and openness. We may improve the emotional effect of our communication and foster a more positive and productive relationship by being aware of the tone in which we speak.

In mindful communication, attentive listening is just as crucial. Giving the speaker our undivided attention, being present and involved, and reacting with compassion and understanding are all components of mindful listening. It necessitates putting electronics like phones and other distractions away and paying close attention to the speaker. By paying close attention, we can have a deeper understanding of the speaker's message, feelings, and needs, which promotes respect for one another.

Active listening is one of the main methods of mindful listening. In addition to hearing what is being said, active listening entails observing the speaker's tone, body language, and emotional indicators. This all-encompassing method of listening enables a deeper comprehension of the speaker's point of view. In addition, active listening entails giving the speaker feedback to demonstrate our interest and engagement, such as by nodding, keeping eye contact, or utilizing vocal affirmations.

Patience training is a critical component of mindful listening. This entails neither hurrying nor interjecting during the speaker's entire expression. It involves being at ease with silences and pauses, allowing the speaker time to gather and express their thoughts. By being patient, we foster a more understanding and encouraging listening atmosphere while demonstrating respect for the speaker's approach.

Using reflective listening is another effective mindful communication strategy. Reflective listening is summarizing or paraphrasing what has been stated to verify our understanding and demonstrate our active participation. Using this method, the speaker can address misunderstandings and make their point more straightforward. Empathy is shown further by reflective listening, which indicates that we are attempting to comprehend the viewpoint and emotions of the speaker.

Apart from employing these strategies, fostering an impartial mindset while conversing is crucial. This entails going into talks with an open mind and no biases or preconceptions. We can promote a more welcoming and inclusive atmosphere where people feel free to express themselves honestly by putting judgment aside. By removing our biases from the conversation, we can ultimately realize the speaker's experiences and feelings, leading to a deeper level of understanding and empathy.

Being conscious of our feelings and responses during talks is another aspect of mindful communication. This self-awareness encourages more deliberate and meaningful communication while averting reactive reactions. We can react consistently with our aims and beliefs by paying attention to our feelings and reactions. This self-control promotes more positive and courteous encounters even in difficult or emotionally charged circumstances.

The development of mindful communication skills can be facilitated by incorporating mindfulness techniques into our daily lives. Techniques like body scanning, deep breathing, and meditation can support the development of presence, awareness, and emotional control. By laying a foundation of mindfulness that can be used for communication, these techniques improve our capacity to pay attention, stay in the moment, and listen carefully and deliberately.

One way to establish a positive and focused tone for the day is to begin with mindfulness meditation. Through consistent practice, we can develop a sense of presence and tranquility to bring to our relationships with other people. Similarly, centering oneself and fostering an atmosphere of openness and receptivity can be achieved by inhaling deeply a few times before starting a conversation.

Establishing a mindful setting can also promote mindful conversation. This entails reducing outside distractions and setting up an environment encouraging presence and concentration. For instance, selecting a peaceful and cozy setting for talks can aid in lowering outside distractions and fostering a more encouraging atmosphere for thoughtful communication. Similarly, establishing limits on technology—for example, by putting away gadgets or turning off notifications—can facilitate the creation of an environment conducive to concentrated and undistracted conversation.

Using self-compassion in communication is another crucial component of mindful communication. This is treating oneself with kindness and compassion, mainly when we make errors or have difficulty communicating. By engaging in self-compassion practices, we can cultivate an environment within ourselves that is more accepting and forgiving, which can improve our capacity for conscious interpersonal communication. In addition to enabling us to recognize our needs and boundaries, self-compassion also fosters a more courteous and balanced communication style.

To sum up, mindful communication is an approach that incorporates mindfulness into our interactions with other people. People can improve their capacity to listen intently, express ideas and feelings clearly, and forge deeper connections by practicing empathy, being present, and letting go of judgment. Techniques for mindful speaking, like pausing before speaking, selecting polite and clear language, and paying attention to tone, can enhance the efficacy and decency of communication. Mutual respect and understanding can be strengthened using reflective listening, active listening, and patience exercises. The development of mindful communication skills can be aided by incorporating mindfulness techniques into daily activities and cultivating a mindful setting. In the end, mindful communication fosters more kind, peaceful, and meaningful interactions, strengthening interpersonal bonds and fostering a more aware and connected society.

Integrating Mindfulness into Routine Tasks

A sense of awareness, presence, and purpose are critical to incorporating mindfulness into daily actions. A standard definition of mindfulness is the ability to completely engage in the present moment without passing judgment. This skill can be skillfully applied to many different facets of daily life. By integrating mindfulness into everyday chores, people can improve their general well-being, lower stress levels, and develop a closer relationship with their experiences. The idea of incorporating mindfulness into ordinary tasks is explored in this section, along with the advantages of doing so and some instances of mindful routines that can be implemented into daily life.

Although mindfulness is frequently connected to structured activities like yoga and meditation, it may also be applied to the routine tasks in our everyday lives. People can turn ordinary tasks into chances for presence and awareness by engaging in mindfulness practices during them. This method shifts the emphasis from just doing duties to living in the present moment to the fullest.

A significant advantage of incorporating mindfulness into daily chores is decreasing tension and anxiety. People are less prone to worry about the past or the future when present. This presence makes it possible to feel more at ease and relaxed, even amid hectic or difficult situations. Moreover, mindfulness fosters attention and clarity, empowering people to approach activities comfortably.

The improvement of general well-being is a crucial advantage of attentive routines. Mindfulness can be incorporated into daily activities to help people appreciate life's small joys more. This appreciation increases feelings of thankfulness and satisfaction, which elevate mood and enhance emotional health. Furthermore, by fostering a sense of harmony and balance in daily life, thoughtful habits can support a happier and healthier way of living.

Mindful eating is one of the easiest ways to incorporate awareness into daily routines. A primary activity, eating is frequently done mindlessly, paying little attention to the sensations or the body's signals of hunger and fullness.

People can turn mealtimes into chances for presence and awareness by engaging in mindful eating. This is being acutely aware of the meal's tastes, textures, and fragrances in addition to the actual physical experience of eating. By acknowledging and respecting the body's cues of hunger and fullness, mindful eating also enables people to have a positive relationship with food.

Walking is another everyday activity that can benefit from mindfulness. Incorporating walking, a primary and natural type of exercise, into daily routines is easy. People can improve their physical and emotional health by engaging in mindful walking. This entails being aware of the sensations experienced when walking, including the feel of the ground beneath the feet, the motion of the legs, and the breathing rhythm. Being aware of the sights, sounds, and smells of one's surroundings is another aspect of mindful walking. By practicing mindfulness, people can turn walking from a mundane pastime into a peaceful and revitalizing experience.

Cleaning, cooking, and laundry are frequently considered tedious and time-consuming. But these pursuits can also present chances to practice mindfulness. For instance, mindful cleaning focuses on the actions and feelings involved in cleaning, such as the satisfaction of having a clean room, the feel of the cloth, and the scent of the cleaning supplies. Similarly, mindful cooking calls for complete attention to every step of the food preparation, from slicing vegetables to stirring pots. People can turn these duties into moments of happiness and presence by applying mindfulness.

Routines for personal hygiene, including washing, shaving, and clothing, can also benefit from mindfulness. These tasks are frequently completed automatically, paying little regard to the body's requirements or the senses. People can improve their well-being and sense of self-care through mindfulness in personal care routines.

When taking a mindful bath, for instance, you should be aware of how the water feels on your skin, the scent of the soap, and how clean you feel. Being mindful of your movements and feelings as you brush your teeth, comb your hair, and apply lotion is part of mindful grooming. Mindfulness can be used in personal care practices to help people feel refreshed and at ease.

Daily commutes are another setting in which mindfulness might be used. Although most people view their commute as a tedious and stressful part of the day, it can also be a chance to practice mindfulness. For instance, mindful driving is giving your concentration to the task at hand, focusing on the road ahead, the sounds of the engine, and the feel of the steering wheel. Similarly, attentive riding on public transit entails paying attention to your environment, ride, and the people you are riding with. By incorporating mindfulness into their commute, people can lower their stress levels and make the journey more pleasant and thoughtful.

Another significant context in which mindfulness can be used is in the workplace and other professional pursuits. Individuals can increase their focus, productivity, and job satisfaction by engaging in mindfulness practices. For instance, mindful working is approaching activities with a sense of purpose and goal, being present in the task, and paying close attention to the details. This entails establishing distinct boundaries between work and leisure time and taking regular pauses to stretch, breathe, and concentrate. People can build a more balanced and contented career by practicing mindfulness at work.

Relationships and social interactions can also incorporate mindfulness. People can improve their relationships with others and have more meaningful and compassionate exchanges by engaging in mindful communication practices. This entails paying close attention during talks, speaking, and giving meaningful answers. Being honest and courteous in one's expression of self, as well as being conscious of the needs and feelings of others, are all components of mindful communication. Through practicing mindfulness in social situations, people can cultivate compassion, understanding, and respect for one another.

Exercise is another everyday activity that might benefit from mindfulness. A healthy lifestyle must include physical activity, and exercising while practicing mindfulness can increase its advantages. For instance, mindful yoga encourages you to be aware of your breath, your body's sensations, and your actions. This practice enhances mental and physical health by fostering harmony and balance. Similarly, mindful running or cycling entails paying attention to your environment, breathing pattern, and body's actions. People can design a more pleasurable and productive exercise regimen by incorporating mindfulness.

Another crucial area where mindfulness can be used is in sleep and rest. Before going to bed, people can enhance the quality of their sleep and have a more peaceful night by engaging in mindfulness practices. For instance, mindful breathing relaxes the body while focusing on the breath. Similarly, mindful visualization is picturing a serene setting like a forest or beach. People can cultivate improved sleep hygiene and a sense of relaxation by incorporating mindfulness into their sleep practices.

Apart from these instances, awareness can be incorporated into numerous other facets of everyday existence. For example, mindful gardening entails giving the act of gardening your whole concentration while focusing on the sensations of the soil, the scent of the plants, and the beauty of the natural world. When you listen to music mindfully, you pay attention to the rhythms, sounds, and feelings it evokes. Engaging fully in the book and paying attention to the words, meanings, and emotions presented are all part of mindful reading. People can make these activities more gratifying and enriching by practicing mindfulness.

Creating a mindful setting is another way to support mindfulness practice. This entails reducing outside distractions and setting up an environment encouraging presence and concentration. For instance, calm and relaxation can be cultivated by creating a peaceful and cozy space for yoga or meditation. Similarly, rearranging and clearing out living areas helps foster a more relaxed, more thoughtful atmosphere. People can improve the quality of their mindfulness practice and advance general well-being by cultivating a mindful atmosphere.

To sum up, incorporating mindfulness into daily chores entails infusing everyday activities with a sense of awareness, presence, and intentionality. Engaging in mindfulness during daily tasks can improve their general well-being, lower their stress levels, and develop a stronger bond with their experiences. Activities that can benefit from mindfulness include mindful eating, walking, cleaning, personal care routines, transportation, work, social interactions, exercise, and sleeping. By integrating mindfulness, people can turn routine jobs into chances for happiness and presence. In addition to supporting mindfulness practice, cultivating a mindful atmosphere can enhance general well-being. In the end, mindfulness in daily activities contributes to developing a more contented, balanced, and attentive existence.

CHAPTER IV

Overcoming Challenges in Mindfulness Practice

Dealing with Distractions

Mindfulness practice, a powerful tool for enhancing mental and emotional well-being, offers numerous benefits such as reduced stress and improved focus. However, it often presents various challenges, especially for beginners. Despite these obstacles, maintaining a consistent mindfulness practice is a worthwhile endeavor. The journey towards mindfulness, though fraught with restlessness, impatience, and self-doubt, can be navigated with the right strategies, leading to a more sustainable and effective practice.

One of the primary challenges in mindfulness practice is dealing with a restless mind. Many individuals struggle to quiet their thoughts and focus on the present moment. This restlessness can be particularly pronounced in the initial stages of practice when the mind is not yet accustomed to being still. It is important to remember that mindfulness is not about achieving a blank mind but observing thoughts without attachment or judgment. Accepting that the mind will wander and gently guiding it back to the present moment can help manage restlessness. Over time, this practice of non-judgmental awareness can reduce mental agitation and enhance the ability to maintain focus.

Impatience is a common hurdle in mindfulness practice, especially in a society that often prioritizes quick results. However, it's important to remember that mindfulness is a lifelong journey, not a quick fix. Celebrating small milestones and recognizing incremental progress can help maintain motivation. Patience and persistence are key, as the benefits of mindfulness often become more apparent with consistent practice over time.

Self-doubt and perfectionism can impede mindfulness practice. It's essential to approach mindfulness with self-compassion and an understanding that there is no right or wrong way to practice. Each individual's experience is unique, and what matters most is the intention and effort put into the practice. Embracing imperfection and viewing challenges as opportunities for growth can transform self-doubt into a source of resilience.

Another significant challenge is finding time for mindfulness in a busy schedule. Modern life is often packed with responsibilities, leaving little room for quiet reflection. Incorporating mindfulness into daily routines can help address this challenge. Mindfulness does not always require lengthy meditation sessions; it can be practiced in small moments throughout the day. For instance, taking a few mindful breaths before starting a task, paying full attention to the taste and texture of food during meals, or practicing mindful walking can integrate mindfulness into everyday activities. By embedding mindfulness into the fabric of daily life, it becomes more sustainable and less dependent on finding large blocks of uninterrupted time.

External distractions can also pose a challenge to mindfulness practice. The constant barrage of notifications from digital devices, noisy environments, and other interruptions can make it challenging to maintain focus. Creating a dedicated and serene space for mindfulness practice can help mitigate these distractions. This space does not need to be elaborate; a quiet corner with minimal disturbances can suffice. Additionally, setting boundaries around this practice time, such as turning off notifications and informing others of the intention to practice mindfulness, can help create a conducive environment for focused attention.

Emotional discomfort is another obstacle that practitioners may encounter. Mindfulness involves inwardly observing one's thoughts and feelings, which can sometimes unearth difficult emotions. Confronting feelings of sadness, anger, or anxiety can be challenging and uncomfortable. However, mindfulness teaches the importance of accepting all emotions without judgment. Viewing these emotions as transient experiences rather than permanent states can help cultivate peace and resilience. Seeking support from a mindfulness teacher or joining a mindfulness group can provide guidance and reassurance during these challenging moments.

Lastly, maintaining motivation for mindfulness practice can be difficult, especially during periods of stress or busyness. When life overwhelms, mindfulness practice may be perceived as another task on a long to-do list. To sustain motivation, reconnecting with the initial reasons for starting the practice is helpful. Reflecting on the benefits experienced, even if subtle, can reinforce the value of mindfulness. Additionally, varying the practice by exploring different techniques, such as guided meditations, body scans, or loving-kindness practices, can keep it engaging and fresh.

Overcoming challenges in mindfulness practice requires patience, persistence, and a compassionate approach. By accepting the natural restlessness of the mind, cultivating patience, embracing imperfection, integrating mindfulness into daily life, creating a conducive environment, accepting emotional discomfort, and maintaining motivation, practitioners can navigate the obstacles that arise on their mindfulness journey. These challenges, while inevitable, can become opportunities for growth and deeper understanding. With dedication and an open heart, mindfulness practice can transform from a challenging endeavor into a profound peace and resilience source.

Dealing with distractions is a fundamental challenge in our fast-paced, technology-driven world. Distractions can hinder productivity, impair our ability to focus and increase stress levels. Understanding common distractions and implementing effective management techniques is essential for maintaining focus and achieving our goals. This section will explore the nature of distractions, identify familiar sources, and provide practical strategies for staying focused.

Distractions can be broadly categorized into external and internal distractions. External distractions originate from our environment, including noises, interruptions, and digital notifications. Internal distractions arise from within us, such as wandering thoughts, worries, and physical discomfort. Both types of distractions can significantly impact our ability to concentrate and complete tasks efficiently.

One of the most prevalent external distractions is noise. Whether it's the sound of traffic, conversations, or background music, noise can disrupt our concentration and make it difficult to focus on the task. Creating a quiet and conducive work environment is crucial to managing noise and distractions. This can be achieved by using noise-canceling headphones, playing white noise or instrumental music, or finding a quiet workspace. Additionally, communicating with others about needing a calm environment can minimize interruptions and create a more focused atmosphere.

Digital notifications are another significant source of external distractions. The constant barrage of emails, messages, and social media notifications can fragment our attention and make it challenging to stay focused. Managing digital distractions involves setting boundaries and implementing strategies to limit their impact. Turning off non-essential notifications, setting specific times to check emails and messages, and using apps or tools that block distracting websites help reduce constant interruptions and allow for more focused work periods.

Interruptions from colleagues, family members, or friends can also disrupt our concentration. These interruptions can be particularly challenging if we work in a shared or open-plan environment. It is essential to establish clear boundaries and communicate them effectively to manage interruptions. Let others know when you need uninterrupted time to work, and consider using visual cues, such as a closed door or a "do not disturb" sign, to signal that you are focusing. Scheduling specific times for collaboration and social interactions can minimize unexpected interruptions and allow for dedicated periods of focused work.

Internal distractions, such as wandering thoughts and worries, can be equally disruptive. Our minds naturally wander, leading us to think about past events, future concerns, or unrelated topics. Managing internal distractions requires cultivating mindfulness and practicing techniques that help redirect our attention back to the task at hand. Mindfulness meditation, for example, can train our minds to stay present and focused. By regularly practicing mindfulness, we can develop greater awareness of our thoughts and learn to gently bring our attention back to the present moment when distractions arise.

Physical discomfort is another common internal distraction that can impede our ability to concentrate. Uncomfortable seating, poor posture, and inadequate lighting can all contribute to physical discomfort and distract us from our work. Ensuring an ergonomic workspace is essential for maintaining focus and preventing physical discomfort. Investing in a comfortable chair, adjusting the height of your desk and computer screen, and ensuring proper lighting can significantly reduce physical distractions and enhance your ability to concentrate.

Procrastination is a pervasive internal distraction that affects many people. It involves delaying tasks and opting for more pleasurable or straightforward activities. Procrastination often stems from feelings of overwhelm, fear of failure, or lack of motivation. To overcome procrastination, breaking tasks into smaller, manageable steps can make them feel less daunting. Setting specific goals, creating a schedule, and using techniques such as the Pomodoro Technique can develop a sense of urgency and accountability, making it easier to stay focused and complete tasks.

The Pomodoro Technique is a time management method that involves working in short, focused intervals, typically 25 minutes, followed by a short break. This technique can help manage external and internal distractions by providing structured work periods and regular breaks. During the focused intervals, eliminate as many distractions as possible and fully immerse yourself in the task. The short breaks allow you to recharge and refocus, preventing burnout and maintaining productivity throughout the day.

Another effective strategy for managing distractions is prioritization. Identifying the most important tasks and focusing on them first can help ensure that critical work gets done, even if distractions arise later. Creating a to-do list and categorizing tasks by priority can provide a clear roadmap for the day and help you stay focused on what matters most. Regularly reviewing and adjusting your priorities enables you to keep on track and adapt to changing circumstances.

Establishing a routine can also help manage distractions and create a sense of structure and predictability. Consistent daily exercise can reduce decision fatigue and make it easier to stay focused. Incorporate regular breaks, physical activity, and time for relaxation into your routine to maintain a healthy balance and prevent burnout. Sticking to a routine can create a rhythm that supports focus and productivity, making it easier to manage distractions and stay on task.

Limiting multitasking is another crucial technique for managing distractions and staying focused. Multitasking may seem like an efficient way to get more done, but it often leads to decreased productivity and increased stress. When we try to juggle multiple tasks simultaneously, our attention becomes fragmented, making us more prone to mistakes and errors. Instead, practice single-tasking by focusing on one task at a time and giving it your full attention. This approach can improve the quality of your work and help you complete tasks more efficiently.

Mindful breaks are an essential part of managing distractions and maintaining focus. Regular breaks can prevent mental fatigue and help you stay refreshed and energized. During breaks, engage in activities promoting relaxation and mental clarity, such as stretching, deep breathing, or walking. Mindful breaks can help you recharge and return to work with renewed focus and concentration. Additionally, incorporating physical activity into your breaks can improve circulation, reduce stress, and enhance cognitive function.

Creating a clutter-free workspace can also help reduce distractions and improve focus. A tidy and organized workspace can minimize visual distractions and create a more conducive environment for concentration. Regularly declutter your workspace and keep only essential items within reach. Organizing your workspace can help you feel more in control and focused, making it easier to stay on task and manage distractions.

Setting boundaries with technology is another crucial aspect of managing distractions. In today's digital age, technology can be both a valuable tool and a significant source of distraction. Establishing boundaries with technology involves being intentional about how and when you use it. Consider setting times for checking emails and social media and avoid using technology during focused work periods. Using tools and apps that limit screen time and block distracting websites can also help you stay focused and reduce the impact of digital distractions.

Practicing self-discipline is critical to managing distractions and staying focused. Self-discipline involves making conscious choices that align with your goals and priorities, even when distractions are tempting. Developing self-discipline requires setting clear goals, creating a plan of action, and holding yourself accountable. Reviewing your progress and celebrating your achievements can help reinforce self-discipline and motivate you. Building self-discipline takes time and practice, but it is crucial for managing distractions and achieving long-term success.

Mindfulness meditation is a powerful technique for managing distractions and improving focus. Mindfulness meditation involves training your mind to stay present and attentive by focusing on your breath, sensations, or a specific object. Regular mindfulness meditation can increase your ability to concentrate, reduce the impact of internal distractions, and enhance your overall well-being. Even a few minutes of mindfulness meditation each day can significantly affect your ability to manage distractions and stay focused.

Creating a positive and supportive work environment can also help manage distractions and improve focus. Surround yourself with people who support your goals and encourage your efforts. Minimizing negative influences and toxic environments can reduce stress and create a more conducive atmosphere for concentration. Building a network of supportive colleagues, friends, and mentors can provide motivation, accountability, and encouragement, helping you stay focused and manage distractions effectively.

In addition to the strategies mentioned, it is essential to recognize that everyone experiences distractions differently. What works for one person may only work for one person. Therefore, it is necessary to experiment with different techniques and find what works best for you. Being flexible and adaptable in your approach can help you tailor your strategies to your unique needs and circumstances, enhancing your ability to manage distractions and stay focused.

In conclusion, dealing with distractions is critical to maintaining focus and achieving our goals in today's fast-paced world. Distractions can be external, such as noise and digital notifications, or internal, such as wandering thoughts and physical discomfort. Managing these distractions requires a combination of practical strategies and mindful techniques. Creating a quiet and conducive work environment, setting boundaries with technology, and practicing mindfulness meditation are effective ways to manage distractions and improve focus. Additionally, establishing a routine, prioritizing tasks, and taking mindful breaks can enhance productivity and prevent burnout. Developing self-discipline, practicing single-tasking, and creating a clutter-free workspace is essential for staying focused and managing distractions. By experimenting with different techniques and finding what works best, you can cultivate the skills to manage distractions effectively and stay focused on your goals.

Handling Difficult Emotions

Handling difficult emotions is a significant challenge for many individuals, yet it is an essential aspect of maintaining mental health and overall well-being. Emotions like anger, sadness, fear, and anxiety are natural human experiences, but when these emotions become overwhelming or persist for extended periods, they can negatively impact one's quality of life. Mindfulness strategies for emotional regulation offer practical tools for processing and understanding these emotions. This section explores the nature of difficult emotions, discusses mindfulness strategies for emotional regulation, and provides exercises to help individuals process and understand their emotions.

Difficult emotions often arise in response to stressful or challenging situations. These emotions can be intense and uncomfortable, prompting various physiological and psychological reactions. For example, anger may cause an increase in heart rate and blood pressure, while sadness might lead to a sense of heaviness or lethargy. Fear and anxiety can trigger a fight-or-flight response, leading to heightened alertness and physical tension. Understanding the triggers and manifestations of these emotions is the first step toward effectively managing them.

Mindfulness, defined as paying attention to the present moment with openness and without judgment, offers a powerful approach to emotional regulation. By cultivating mindfulness, individuals can become more aware of their emotional states, recognize their triggers, and respond to their emotions in healthier ways. Mindfulness helps to create a space between the experience of an emotion and the reaction to it, allowing for a more thoughtful and measured response.

One of the primary mindfulness strategies for emotional regulation is observing emotions without judgment. This involves acknowledging the presence of the emotion without labeling it as good or bad. By observing emotions in this way, individuals can gain insight into the nature of their emotional experiences and reduce the tendency to react impulsively. For example, when feeling anger, one might note, "I am experiencing anger," rather than immediately acting on the emotion. This practice helps to cultivate a sense of detachment and serenity, allowing individuals to respond to their feelings with greater clarity and wisdom.

Another key mindfulness strategy is the practice of acceptance. Acceptance involves allowing emotions to be present without trying to suppress or avoid them. This can be challenging, especially with difficult emotions, but it is essential for emotional regulation. Suppressing feelings can lead to increased tension and long-term psychological issues, while avoidance can prevent individuals from addressing the underlying causes of their feelings. By accepting emotions as they arise, individuals can begin to process and understand them more fully. This practice helps create a sense of inner peace and resilience as individuals learn to navigate their emotional landscape more easily.

Breathing exercises are a practical mindfulness technique that can help regulate emotions. Deep, mindful breathing activates the parasympathetic nervous system, promoting relaxation and reducing stress and anxiety's physiological symptoms. One effective exercise is diaphragmatic breathing, where individuals focus on breathing deeply into the diaphragm, allowing the belly to rise and fall with each breath. This type of breathing can help to calm the mind and body, making it easier to manage difficult emotions. Another helpful technique is the 4-7-8 breathing exercise, which involves inhaling for a count of four, holding the breath for a count of seven, and exhaling for a count of eight. This exercise helps slow the breathing rate and promote a sense of calm.

Body scan meditation is another mindfulness practice that can help individuals become more aware of their emotional and physical states. This exercise involves systematically focusing attention on different parts of the body, starting from the toes and moving up to the head. As individuals scan each part of the body, they are encouraged to notice any sensations, tension, or discomfort without judgment. This practice helps to cultivate a greater awareness of the connection between the body and emotions, allowing individuals to identify and address areas of tension or stress. By regularly practicing body scan meditation, individuals can develop a greater sense of bodily awareness and emotional regulation.

Mindful movement practices like yoga or tai chi can also benefit emotional regulation. These practices combine physical movement with conscious awareness, helping individuals to connect with their bodies and release emotional tension. For example, yoga involves a series of postures and breathwork that promote relaxation and balance. Through mindful movement, individuals can learn to listen to their bodies and emotions, allowing for a more integrated approach to emotional regulation. These practices also help build resilience and flexibility, physically and emotionally, making it easier to handle difficult emotions.

Mindfulness-based cognitive therapy (MBCT) is a structured approach that combines mindfulness practices with cognitive behavioral techniques to help individuals manage difficult emotions. MBCT helps individuals identify and challenge negative thought patterns contributing to emotional distress. Individuals can develop a more balanced and compassionate perspective by bringing mindful awareness to these thoughts. For example, if someone is experiencing anxiety about a future event, they might use mindfulness to observe their anxious thoughts without getting caught up in them. They can then use cognitive techniques to reframe these thoughts in a more positive and realistic light. MBCT is effective in reducing symptoms of depression, anxiety, and other emotional disorders.

Loving-kindness meditation is another mindfulness practice that can help to regulate difficult emotions. This practice involves cultivating feelings of compassion and kindness towards oneself and others. Individuals can counterbalance negative emotional states by focusing on positive emotions and developing a greater sense of emotional well-being. Loving-kindness meditation typically involves repeating phrases such as "May I be happy, may I be healthy, may I be safe, may I live with ease" and extending these wishes to others. This practice helps to foster a sense of connection and empathy, making it easier to manage difficult emotions with compassion and understanding.

In addition to these mindfulness practices, developing healthy coping strategies for dealing with difficult emotions is essential. This might include engaging in activities promoting relaxation and well-being, such as leisure time in nature, listening to music, or practicing creative arts. Physical exercise is also a powerful tool for emotional regulation, as it helps to release endorphins and reduce stress. Maintaining a balanced lifestyle, with adequate sleep, nutrition, and social support, is essential for managing emotions effectively.

Journaling is another valuable exercise for processing and understanding emotions. Writing about one's emotional experiences helps clarify thoughts and feelings, making it easier to gain insight and perspective. Journaling provides a safe and private space to explore emotions, identify patterns, and develop coping strategies. For example, individuals might write about a recent experience that triggered a problematic feeling, examine the thoughts and beliefs associated with that emotion, and consider alternative ways of responding. This practice helps to promote self-awareness and emotional intelligence, making it easier to navigate challenging emotional landscapes.

Another helpful exercise is the practice of gratitude. Focusing on positive aspects of life can shift attention away from difficult emotions and promote a more balanced emotional state. Keeping a gratitude journal, where individuals regularly write down things they are grateful for, can help to cultivate a sense of appreciation and positivity. This practice helps counterbalance negative emotions and promote a more optimistic outlook.

Developing a support network is also crucial for handling difficult emotions. Sharing experiences and feelings with trusted friends, family members, or a therapist can provide valuable support and perspective. Talking about emotions helps reduce their intensity and can provide insights into managing them more effectively. Seeking professional help, such as therapy or counseling, can also provide structured support and guidance for managing difficult emotions. Therapists can offer techniques and strategies for emotional regulation and help individuals develop healthier coping methods.

In conclusion, handling difficult emotions is a complex but essential aspect of maintaining mental health and well-being. Mindfulness strategies for emotional regulation, such as observing emotions without judgment, practicing acceptance, and using breathing exercises, offer practical tools for managing emotions. Mindful movement practices, mindfulness-based cognitive therapy, and loving-kindness meditation provide additional support for emotional regulation. Developing healthy coping strategies, such as engaging in relaxation activities, journaling, practicing gratitude, and seeking social support, can further enhance one's ability to process and understand emotions. By incorporating these mindfulness practices and coping strategies into daily life, individuals can navigate their emotional landscape with greater ease and resilience, improving their emotional well-being and overall quality of life.

Building Consistency

Many people have turned to mindfulness in today's fast-paced society to achieve emotional balance and mental peace. This mindfulness technique, which strongly emphasizes being in the present, has several advantages, from lowered stress levels to enhanced general well-being. For many people, nevertheless, the difficulty is in developing a consistent and long-lasting mindfulness practice. Consistent mindfulness practice requires commitment, tolerance, and a few calculated moves. This section provides insights and advice to ensure the sustainability of mindfulness practice by examining different approaches to starting and keeping up a regular practice.

First things first, it's critical to comprehend the significance of mindfulness. Beyond merely a catchphrase, mindfulness is a scientifically validated approach that improves mental clarity, emotional stability, and physical well-being. Regular mindfulness practice has been linked to lowered blood pressure, enhanced cognitive performance, and a reduction in the symptoms of depression and anxiety, according to studies. Acknowledging these advantages can be a strong incentive to stick with the practice. Prioritizing and incorporating mindfulness into everyday activities is made more accessible when one is aware of its significant effects on one's life.

Setting specific, attainable goals is the first step in developing a regular mindfulness practice. Often, the idea of long-term meditation might be intimidating to novices. It's crucial to begin slowly and extend the duration progressively as you get more comfortable. To make the practice less intimidating and more achievable, try starting with just five minutes daily and gradually increasing it. Establishing measurable objectives, like meditating for 10 minutes each morning, can provide one direction and a sense of accomplishment as they are reached.

Establishing a specific area for practicing mindfulness can significantly improve consistency. An environment that is calm, cozy, and distraction-free can aid in alerting the mind when it is time to turn inside. This area doesn't have to be fancy; it is a chair or cushion in the corner of the room, maybe with some plants or candles for ambiance. Setting aside a specific space for mindfulness can aid in creating a routine and integrating the practice into everyday activities.

Adding attention to routine tasks is another powerful strategy for developing consistency. It is possible to incorporate mindfulness into many facets of daily life, not limited to structured meditation sessions. Giving complete attention to the sensations and experiences in the present now, even seemingly simple things like eating, walking, or even brushing your teeth may be turned into mindfulness exercises. By connecting mindfulness with daily duties, this method not only increases accessibility to the practice but also aids in habit reinforcement.

Having accountability can help continue a regular mindfulness practice. Joining a mindfulness group or discussing your objectives with a friend can help you get the support and motivation you need to keep moving forward. Adding fresh viewpoints and methods to one's practice while practicing with others might enhance one's journey toward mindfulness. Monitoring tools or apps for mindfulness can also help keep track of progress and act as a reminder to practice regularly. These tools frequently provide guided sessions and prompts to maintain an exciting and varied practice.

Building any new habit, including mindfulness, naturally involves overcoming challenges and resolving setbacks. It's critical to handle these difficulties with compassion and without bias. There will be days when practicing is challenging due to time constraints or restless thoughts. Resilience and tenacity can be fostered by accepting these moments rather than giving up and gradually returning to the practice. Recognizing that practicing mindfulness is a journey with ups and downs might help keep one's motivation and frustration levels low.

Maintaining a thoughtful attitude all day can also help ensure the practice's sustainability. This calls for being alert and always in the moment, no matter what you're doing. One can cultivate a more aware lifestyle by incorporating mindfulness into daily interactions, professional settings, and recreational pursuits. Practicing mindfulness consistently can help it become ingrained in your life and not just a one-time event.

To create a meaningful and long-lasting practice, it is necessary to investigate the deeper facets of mindfulness in addition to these valuable pointers. Buddhism and other ancient contemplative traditions, which strongly emphasize developing awareness and compassion, are the origins of mindfulness. Gaining insight into the philosophical underpinnings of mindfulness can enhance the practice's context and depth. Engaging in workshops, retreats, or book reading can provide insightful knowledge and motivation. Developing ties with the larger mindfulness community can also help people feel they have a common goal and place.

Sustaining a consistent mindfulness routine necessitates continuous dedication and flexibility. Because life is dynamic and situations change frequently, practicing regularly might be difficult. It is essential to be adaptable and open to modifying the practice to suit various life stages and circumstances. For instance, shorter but more frequent mindfulness exercises may be more practical during periods of high stress or busyness. On the other hand, longer and more focused practice sessions may be advantageous during slower times. Maintaining the practice's relevance and continuity can be facilitated by tailoring it to an individual's needs and circumstances.

Lastly, thinking back on the development and advantages of mindfulness practice helps strengthen the resolve to stick with it. Being able to consistently recognize and value the improvements in one's physical, mental, and emotional health can be a highly effective motivator. Maintaining a mindfulness diary to record experiences and realizations can serve as a concrete progress log and a helpful reminder of the practice's worth. Resolve and morale can be strengthened by identifying and appreciating little victories and the work required to keep up the practice.

In summary, developing a consistent and long-lasting mindfulness practice requires commitment, tolerance, and thoughtful preparation. One can build a strong and long-lasting practice by comprehending the advantages of mindfulness, establishing reasonable objectives, designating a specific area, integrating mindfulness into everyday activities, asking for accountability, overcoming challenges with compassion, developing a mindful attitude, investigating the more profound facets of mindfulness, adjusting to shifting conditions, and thinking back on personal development. A fuller, more satisfying existence results from practicing mindfulness every moment of the day. It is a journey rather than a destination. A sustainable mindfulness practice can become the foundation of well-being and inner serenity with perseverance and a caring attitude.

Addressing Resistance and Doubt

Resistance and uncertainty are among the most common and significant challenges in personal development or adopting new practices, like mindfulness or self-improvement. Humans naturally react with resistance and doubt to change or novel concepts. Comprehending these reactions and acquiring coping mechanisms for personal development and goal achievement is essential. This section examines the nature of doubt and resistance to their causes and offers strategies for dealing with and overcoming them.

Procrastination, avoidance, or an overall lack of motivation are common ways resistance shows up. It is a psychological safeguard that aids people in avoiding discomfort or imagined dangers. Conversely, doubt is the absence of conviction or confusion about something. It may be the result of prior bad experiences, ignorance, or fear of failing. Doubt and resistance combined can erect formidable obstacles to growth and development.

Fear of the unknown is one of the leading causes of resistance. When confronted with novel concepts or alterations, the human mind tends to return to known patterns and routines. This results from the brain's innate desire for stability and safety. In contrast, people view the unknown as harmful and risky. People may resist because they would rather stay in their comfort zones than go to new places due to this innate dread.

Self-doubt is another prevalent source of resistance. People may need to be more confident in implementing new procedures or making adjustments successfully. This may be especially true if prior endeavors have failed or disappointed you. Self-doubt can set off a negative feedback loop in which avoidance behaviors are motivated by the fear of failing, which feeds the feeling that one is inadequate.

Societal and cultural factors can also influence doubt and resistance. Individual attitudes and perceptions about change can be influenced by societal norms and expectations. For example, there may be a greater aversion to new ideas and behaviors in cultures that emphasize tradition and stability. Furthermore, societal pressures and judgments can make people's self-doubt worse because they may fear rejection or criticism from others.

It is crucial to recognize and comprehend resistance before attempting to overcome it. To do this, one must examine themselves and determine which particular fears or beliefs are causing the resistance. By raising these underlying factors to the level of consciousness, people might question and refute them. For instance, reframe failure as an opportunity for progress rather than a threat by realizing that it is a natural part of the learning process and that dread of it is usual.

Gradual exposure is a valuable strategy for getting over resistance. This entails moving toward the intended change or new activity in tiny, gradual steps. People can lessen their sense of peril and eventually gain confidence by segmenting the procedure into manageable pieces. For example, if someone is reluctant to start a new fitness regimen, they can start with quick, easy workouts and progressively increase the length and intensity over time. Taking this strategy, the change may gain traction and seem less daunting.

Another crucial tactic is to foster a growth attitude. A growth mindset is a conviction that skills and intelligence can be acquired via work and education instead of a fixed attitude. Adopting a growth mindset enables people to see obstacles and failures as chances for personal improvement instead of proof of their limits. This change in viewpoint can lessen resistance and self-doubt, facilitating the adoption of novel concepts and methods.

Positive thinking and visualization are two more effective methods for getting past resistance. Visualization is successfully imagining oneself carrying out the intended action or accomplishing the objective. This mental practice helps lessen change-related anxiety and boost confidence. Conversely, positive affirmations entail saying things that are empowering and supportive to oneself. Getting over reluctance and doubt can be simpler when you use these affirmations to support a positive self-image and counteract negative self-talk.

Getting assistance from others is essential when dealing with resistance. Friends, family, mentors, or support groups can offer this assistance by providing motivation, responsibility, and perspective. Loneliness can be reduced, and a sense of community can be fostered by talking to others about one's objectives and difficulties.

Furthermore, gaining knowledge and inspiration from those who have effectively managed comparable transitions can be beneficial.

Overcoming doubt and skepticism also requires knowledge and education. Uncertainty frequently results from ignorance of novel concepts or procedures. People can lessen uncertainty and develop more informed perspectives by learning more and finding trustworthy information. This may entail talking to professionals in the industry, attending workshops, or reading literature. It gets simpler to overcome uncertainty and confidently make judgments the more educated one is.

Self-awareness and mindfulness exercises can also significantly aid resistance and skepticism. Being mindful entails focusing on the here and now while maintaining an accepting and open mindset. People who engage in this technique are more conscious of their feelings and ideas, especially those associated with resistance and skepticism. People can establish a distance between their ideas and behaviors by monitoring these emotions without passing judgment. This space enables more deliberate and less reactive replies. The root reasons for resistance and uncertainty can be found and addressed with this enhanced self-awareness.

To help overcome resistance and skepticism, cognitive-behavioral approaches can be used in addition to mindfulness. Cognitive-behavioral therapy, or CBT, aims to recognize and question harmful thought patterns and beliefs. People can learn to think more rationally and constructively by identifying and challenging unreasonable or dangerous ideas. For instance, if someone says they can't succeed at a new task, they can examine the evidence and explore other possibilities to refute this idea. This procedure can assist in lowering self-doubt and boosting self-assurance in one's skills.

Overcoming resistance also requires establishing a favorable and encouraging environment. This can entail setting up routines and habits that support the intended transformation, as well as arranging one's actual surroundings to minimize distractions and increase focus. Suppose someone is attempting to start a regular meditation practice, for instance. In that case, they can designate a peaceful and cozy area for meditation and construct a daily schedule that includes a specified time for practice. A supportive setting might lessen resistance by facilitating and reinforcing the new behavior.

Another essential element in dealing with resistance and skepticism is self-compassion. This entails being gentle and understanding to oneself, particularly while facing difficulties and disappointments. Self-compassion can offset the severe self-criticism that frequently accompanies resistance and self-doubt. People can foster a more positive and caring internal environment supporting transformation and growth by practicing self-compassion and forgiveness.

Overcoming opposition and uncertainty also requires patience and persistence. Since change is frequently a protracted process, roadblocks and setbacks are commonplace. Remaining dedicated to the process and watching the big picture is crucial. Rewarding modest accomplishments and advancements may keep momentum and drive high. People can maintain their resilience and persistence by realizing that resistance and doubt are standard components of the transformation process.

In summary, dealing with resistance and doubt necessitates a multimodal strategy that includes self-analysis, gradual exposure, developing a growth mindset, visualization, asking for help, education, mindfulness, CBT, building a nurturing environment, self-compassion, and perseverance. By comprehending the characteristics and sources of resistance and uncertainty, people can create efficient plans to overcome these obstacles and accomplish their objectives. It takes more than just implementing new habits to overcome resistance and doubt—one must also change how one thinks about, and approaches change. People can overcome reluctance and doubt with commitment and the appropriate techniques, which promote personal development, boost confidence and result in a more satisfying existence.

CHAPTER V

Deepening Your Mindfulness Practice

Expanding Awareness

Deepening one's mindfulness practice requires increasing awareness and extending the practice's boundaries. Fundamentally, mindfulness is being open-minded and curious while paying attention to the current moment. Still, its possibilities go far beyond merely being aware of the here and now. By extending mindfulness practice, people can develop a better awareness of themselves and the world around them, improve their emotional intelligence, and promote greater well-being. This section will examine the idea of increasing awareness, review several mindfulness practices with this aim, and emphasize the advantages of a more comprehensive mindfulness practice.

The first step toward expanding awareness is realizing that mindfulness is not confined to meditation. Even though it's a very effective method, meditation is just one part of a more comprehensive mindfulness practice. Bringing mindfulness into everyday activities like eating, walking, and socializing is critical to expanding awareness. By doing this, People can cultivate a more comprehensive and integrated mindfulness practice.

Eating with awareness can be one approach to increased awareness. This practice entails focusing on food's flavor, texture, and scent and the whole sensory experience of eating. Eating mindfully helps people appreciate every bite, pay attention to bodily sensations, and identify when hungry or full. This practice can result in a better appreciation of food, better digestion, and a positive relationship with eating. Furthermore, mindful eating can assist people in developing a better awareness of their body requirements and making more deliberate decisions about what and how much to consume.

Mindful walking is another effective way to increase awareness. This practice entails walking with conscious attention and paying attention to the feelings in the legs and feet, the breathing pattern, and the surroundings. You can practice mindful walking anywhere—in the city, outdoors, or indoors. People who engage in this technique report feeling more connected to their body, less stressed, and more present and grounded. Walking mindfully can also help cultivate a sense of wonder and appreciation for the natural world by fostering a closer bond with the environment and nature.

Mindful listening is another method for increasing awareness. This exercise entails paying close attention to noises around you, in music, and during interactions with others. To listen mindfully, one must put aside preconceived notions and outside distractions and concentrate solely on the sounds and the auditory experience. This exercise can strengthen relationships, increase communication, and promote a more profound sense of empathy and connection. People can develop a greater awareness of the subtleties of sound and the feelings and intentions underlying speech by practicing attentive listening.

Meditation using the body scan technique is another valuable tool for raising awareness. This technique methodically focuses on various body parts, noting tension, sensations, and relaxing spots. The body scan usually starts at the feet and works its way up to the head, and it can be performed while sitting or lying down. Through this exercise, people can induce relaxation, reduce physical tension, and become more conscious of their body's sensations. Additionally, the body scan can strengthen the link between the mind and body, making people more aware of their mental and physical situations.

Metta meditation, another name for loving-kindness meditation, is a potent technique for developing compassion and raising consciousness. This meditation aims to create feelings of love and kindness for oneself, as well as for loved ones, acquaintances, and even people with whom one has trouble. Usually, the exercise entails repeating positive affirmations to yourself and others, such as "May I be happy, may I be healthy, may I be safe." Meditation with loving-kindness can improve emotional resilience, lessen unpleasant emotions, and cultivate a stronger sense of empathy and connection with others.

Practicing mindfulness with one's thoughts and emotions is another way to broaden awareness. This is the technique of objectively and dispassionately aware of thoughts and feelings as they emerge. People can gain a better sense of perspective and detachment by realizing that thoughts and feelings are just fleeting mental occurrences. This technique can improve general mental health by promoting emotional regulation, lessening the effects of unpleasant thoughts and feelings, and enhancing emotional control. Whether in meditation or daily life, mindfulness of thoughts and emotions can be developed by periodically checking in with oneself and observing the inner experience.

Creating with awareness in mind is another method to increase awareness. This gives creative endeavors like writing, painting, music-making, and drawing deliberate attention. Mindful creation encourages people to let go of expectations and judgments, notice the feelings and sensations that arise, and immerse themselves in the creative process. This exercise can improve flow and presence, lessen tension, and boost creativity. People who practice mindful creation can also connect with their inner selves and express themselves authentically.

Cultivating mindfulness in interpersonal relationships is another crucial component of increasing awareness. This is being present, paying close attention to interactions, and reacting compassionately and understanding. Active listening, honest and straightforward self-expression, and awareness of body language and nonverbal clues are all components of mindful communication. People can improve their communication, develop more potent and more meaningful connections with others, and increase their emotional intelligence by engaging in mindfulness practices in their relationships.

Including mindfulness in regular tasks and routines is another powerful strategy to increase awareness. This can entail approaching routine activities like driving, doing the dishes, and brushing your teeth with awareness. Those who participate entirely in these activities and pay attention to their surroundings, movements, and sensations can turn ordinary tasks into chances to practice mindfulness. This method assists in incorporating mindfulness into everyday activities to become a regular and organic part of a person's schedule.

Developing a more profound, comprehensive sense of the present is one of the main advantages of increasing consciousness through mindfulness. People grow more aware of their inner experiences and the outside environment when they apply mindfulness to many facets of their existence. Increased awareness might result from increased self-awareness, improved emotional control, and a heightened appreciation of the present moment. Additionally, it can foster compassion for oneself and others and a sense of oneness.

Increasing awareness can also significantly affect one's physical and emotional well-being. Studies have demonstrated that mindfulness exercises help lessen stress, lessen the signs of anxiety and depression, and enhance general well-being. By integrating mindfulness practices into their daily lives, people can cultivate a more harmonious and balanced way of living that promotes their mental and physical well-being. For instance, mindful movement techniques like yoga or tai chi can increase flexibility and physical fitness, while mindful eating can encourage better eating habits and improve digestion.

Moreover, practicing mindfulness to increase awareness can encourage more creativity and innovation. People can approach issues and difficulties differently by fostering openness and curiosity. A nonjudgmental mindset is fostered by mindfulness, which facilitates the investigation of novel concepts and more imaginative thought. This can be especially helpful in academic and professional contexts where original thought and creative problem-solving are highly regarded.

Increasing awareness through mindfulness can have significant effects on social interactions and interpersonal connections in addition to personal benefits. A person can develop more profound and lasting relationships with others by engaging in mindful communication and exercising empathy. This can foster a more caring and compassionate community, improve cooperation, and lessen conflict. A more empathetic and loving society can also benefit from mindfulness techniques that promote compassion and loving-kindness.

Increasing awareness via mindfulness is consistent with environmental conscience and sustainability. People can make more ecologically friendly decisions by developing a closer relationship with the natural world and a better understanding of the effects of their actions. A sense of stewardship and accountability towards the environment can be fostered by engaging in mindful activities like mindful walking outdoors or mindful consumption. Natural resource protection and more sustainable lives may result from this.

In summary, combining multiple mindfulness practices and integrating mindfulness into numerous elements of daily life are vital components of raising awareness and increasing the scope of mindfulness. By doing this, people can better understand the outside world and themselves, improve their emotional intelligence, and advance overall well-being. Expanding awareness can be facilitated by engaging in mindfulness techniques like mindful eating, mindful walking, mindful conversation, body scan meditation, loving-kindness meditation, mindful eating, mindful creativity, and mindful communication. Increased creativity and inventiveness, better mental and physical health, stronger relationships, and a more compassionate and sustainable lifestyle are all advantages of a more extensive mindfulness practice. People can change their lives and make a difference in the world by adopting a more holistic approach to mindfulness.

Mindfulness in Relationships

A deep strategy for improving relationships is mindfulness, which calls for giving conversations with people your whole attention and presence. People can improve connection, empathy, and relationship quality by implementing mindfulness in their relationships. Present, non-judgmental, and compassionate tenets form the foundation of mindful relationships and promote a greater understanding and respect of one another. This section examines the idea of mindfulness in relationships, its advantages, and the several techniques that can be used to foster empathic and attentive partnerships.

Fundamentally, mindfulness is being open-minded and curious while paying attention to the current moment. In terms of interpersonal interactions, mindfulness refers to paying close attention to what other people are saying, listening intently, and reacting in a kind and considerate way. This degree of focus can strengthen emotional ties and greatly enhance the quality of encounters. Mutual respect, attentive listening, and understanding one another's feelings and experiences are traits of mindful relationships.

Improved communication is one of mindfulness' main relationship benefits. Healthy relationships are built on effective communication, and mindfulness can significantly enhance our ability to communicate. Being mindful in communication means paying close attention to what the other person is saying without interrupting or thinking of a way to respond. Active listening enables people to genuinely get the other person's viewpoint and provide well-considered responses. People can prevent misunderstandings, lessen disputes, and promote honest and open communication by giving their entire attention and presence during conversations.

Another essential component of conscious partnerships is empathy. Understanding and feeling another person's emotions is a necessary component of empathy. Being more aware of one's feelings as well as those of others is one way that mindfulness can improve empathy. People who practice mindfulness can become more emotionally sensitive and aware, enhancing their ability to respond to their partners' needs and feelings lovingly. This attitude can improve emotional ties and foster a more loving and caring relationship environment.

Mindful breathing is an essential technique for developing mindfulness in relationships. Breathing mindfully entails focusing on the breath and using it as a grounding force to remain in the moment. Taking a few deep breaths can help one center themselves and approach the engagement with a calm and focused mind before starting a conversation or during a quarrel. Doing so can avoid reactive actions, and a more calculated and deliberate approach can be encouraged. In addition to helping people remain grounded and in the moment during interactions, mindful breathing can improve the quality of those exchanges.

Loving-kindness meditation is another beneficial technique for cultivating attentive connections. Metta meditation, also known as loving-kindness meditation, focuses on cultivating compassion and love for oneself and others. This technique develops a feeling of benevolence and positive esteem for one's partner, which can be very helpful in partnerships. They silently repeat self- and partner-instructed wishes, such as "May you be happy, may you be healthy, may you be safe," during loving-kindness meditation. By cultivating a more sympathetic and caring mindset, this activity helps improve partners' emotional bond.

Another effective strategy to improve mindfulness in relationships is mindful touch. A key component of human connection is physical touch, which can increase intimacy and create a feeling of closeness when done thoughtfully. Being completely present and focused when touching or touching is a necessary component of mindful contact. Simple acts like holding hands, offering a hug, or giving a light massage can do this. People can strengthen their relationships and display affection by concentrating on the feelings and emotional connections experienced during these times. Additionally, mindful contact can ease tension and encourage relaxation, which improves relationships.

Another crucial component of mindfulness in relationships is cultivating appreciation. Experiencing gratitude is realizing and valuing the good things in your relationship and your partner. By practicing mindfulness, people can increase their awareness of their relationships' qualities, which can lead to a feeling of satisfaction and gratitude. Frequent expressions of thankfulness can improve the emotional connection between partners and foster a happy, encouraging relationship environment. This can be as easy as setting out some time every day to thank your partner for something they have done or for a trait you find admirable in them.

Any relationship will inevitably involve conflict resolution, and successful conflict management can be significantly aided by mindfulness. Finding solutions that all parties can agree on requires mindful conflict resolution, which entails approaching arguments with composure and an open mind. People can avoid reactive responses and concentrate on finding a constructive solution by being in the moment and refraining from passing judgment. More positive outcomes and a stronger relationship can result from partners navigating disagreements with increased tolerance, understanding, and compassion when they practice mindfulness.

Building mindful partnerships also requires developing attentive self-awareness. Understanding one's feelings, ideas, and behaviors and how they affect relationships is necessary for self-awareness. Through the practice of mindfulness, people can become more self-aware and identify behavioral patterns that might be harmful to their relationships. People with this awareness can consciously choose how they react to their partners and control their emotions. People who practice mindful self-awareness can better control their emotions, break bad habits, and create happier, more harmonious relationships.

Apart from these routines, regular relationship activities might incorporate mindfulness. Mindfulness can be cultivated through simple activities like eating together, taking a stroll, or spending quality time with one another. People can strengthen their bonds and have significant shared experiences by giving these activities their complete attention and presence. Mindfulness can improve the relationship's overall quality by transforming routine moments into chances for greater appreciation and connection.

Beyond one's happiness and well-being, relationships can benefit from mindfulness. Studies have indicated that practicing mindfulness can lower stress, increase relationship satisfaction, and improve the general quality of relationships. Increased emotional connection, reciprocal support, and trust are traits of mindful relationships. People who practice mindfulness can build more satisfying and harmonious relationships that benefit both parties and enhance their general happiness and well-being.

Additionally, cultivating mindfulness in interpersonal interactions can benefit the larger societal context. The foundation of mindful partnerships is empathy, compassion, and nonjudgment; these qualities can affect interactions with people outside of immediate collaboration. People can develop these traits in themselves and serve as role models for others by engaging in mindfulness practices in relationships, which will help create a more compassionate and empathic society. Mindful interactions have the potential to create a more supportive and cohesive community where people feel appreciated and understood.

To sum up, practicing mindfulness in relationships entails giving conversations with people your whole attention and presence to improve connection, empathy, and the general quality of your relationships. People can enhance their ability to communicate, grow more empathetic, and foster loving and supportive relationships by engaging in mindfulness practices. Cultivating mindful connections can benefit from using several mindful practices, including active listening, conscious breathing, loving-kindness meditation, mindful touch, gratitude, mindful conflict resolution, and attentive self-awareness. Beyond improving one's well-being, relationship mindfulness fosters more profound emotional closeness, mutual trust, and support. People can turn routine times into chances for greater appreciation and connection by incorporating mindfulness into their regular relationship activities. A more compassionate and empathic society can be promoted by the beneficial effects of mindfulness in relationships, which can also be seen in the larger social context. People can build happier, more harmonious relationships that benefit both parties and enhance their general well-being by practicing mindfulness.

Exploring Advanced Mindfulness Techniques

Studying more sophisticated mindfulness practices leads to a more profound and profound sense of presence and awareness. While foundational mindfulness exercises like body scans and mindful breathing are essential, more complex methods can enrich and broaden the practice and help people develop a more profound sense of awareness. To assist people in furthering their mindfulness journeys, this section presents a variety of advanced practices, examines advanced mindfulness techniques, and offers guided exercises.

The foundation of fundamental mindfulness practices is frequently strengthened by advanced mindfulness techniques, which delve deeper into the nuances of awareness and the nature of the mind. Vipassana, or insight meditation, is one such method. By noticing the impermanence, unsatisfaction, and selflessness of all occurrences, insight meditation seeks to build a profound understanding of the nature of reality, in contrast to fundamental mindfulness practices that concentrate primarily on cultivating present-moment awareness. In this technique, thoughts, feelings, and sensory sensations are continuously and intently observed as they arise and pass. By developing this profound understanding, practitioners can attain more clarity, calmness, and freedom from mental pain.

Choiceless Awareness is another sophisticated mindfulness technique. By utilizing this approach, practitioners don't fixate on anything; instead, they stay open and alert to whatever comes into their field of awareness. Because the mind tends to dwell on specific objects or thoughts regularly, this practice calls for a high level of understanding and composure. Choiceless Awareness promotes a non-discriminatory and inclusive approach to mindfulness, enabling practitioners to cultivate a more expanded and wide-ranging awareness. This method can promote a more profound sense of openness and presence by assisting people in escaping automatic thought and behavior patterns.

Advanced practitioners can also use sustained Attention techniques. This entails focusing on a single item nonstop for a considerable time. Often used focal points are the breath, a mantra, or an image, like a candle flame —practices involving sustained attention demand high focus and mental stability. People can attain deeper stages of meditative absorption known as Jhanas, improve mental clarity, and lessen mind-wandering by practicing the ability to sustain attention. These intensely focused and peaceful moods can bring life-changing events and insights.

Advanced study can also be done on loving-kindness meditation. Advanced loving-kindness meditation practice methodically expands these feelings to all beings, including those with conflicts or difficulties. Basic loving-kindness meditation involves cultivating love and compassion towards oneself and others. This practice aims to help practitioners develop unconditional love and compassion while overcoming aversion. Proficient in loving-kindness meditation can bring about significant transformations in an individual's mindset and conduct, cultivating increased compassion, understanding, and a feeling of unity with all living things.

Another sophisticated method that entails a thorough and sophisticated investigation of emotional events is mindfulness of emotions. This practice involves learning about the underlying reasons and situations that give rise to emotions, comprehending their fleeting nature, and practicing appropriate responses instead of merely seeing emotions as they come and go. Higher emotional awareness can assist people in escaping reactive behaviors and gaining more emotional balance and resilience. In addition to promoting increased self-awareness and emotional intelligence, this exercise can help people better grasp the interactions between ideas, feelings, and bodily sensations.

Advanced body scan techniques require more in-depth and sophisticated knowledge of physical sensations. Through meticulous attention to various body areas, participants in this exercise notice energetic patterns and subtle sensations. Increased physical and mental well-being, a closer relationship with one's body, and the release of tension and stress can all be achieved with advanced body scan techniques. Additionally, by strengthening the mind-body link, this practice can support a comprehensive view of balance and health.

The Open Monitoring approach is another advanced mindfulness method. This entails remaining open-minded and inclusive while focusing on the current moment without concentrating on any one thing in particular. To let events come and go without attachment or aversion, practitioners maintain an open and receptive state to all kinds of experiences, including ideas, feelings, and sensory sensations. Open Monitoring necessitates a high degree of composure and concentration because the mind is prone to reaction patterns or habitually focusing on particular objects. People who engage in this technique may develop a strong sense of spaciousness and presence, enabling them to appreciate the present moment's richness fully.

Practitioners of advanced mindfulness can also participate in contemplative inquiry. This entails using extended contemplation and meditation to delve into profound concerns regarding the nature of the mind, self, and reality. Practitioners are encouraged by contemplative inquiry to examine their experiences, presumptions, and beliefs with an open mind. This practice can result in a deeper awareness of oneself and the world. Additionally, it can stimulate awe and curiosity, leading to a broader and more unbiased outlook on life.

People can explore these advanced strategies and develop their practice with guided advanced mindfulness activities. The practice of insight meditation is one such activity. Choose a spot to sit that is both peaceful and cozy to start. Shut your eyes and inhale deeply several times to bring yourself into the present. Please focus on the breath and notice how it feels entering and exiting the body. As you settle in, begin to include thoughts, feelings, and sense experiences in your awareness. Watch for these occurrences and observe how fleeting and temporary they are. Just observe whatever comes up with curiosity and composure, allowing your awareness to be inclusive and nonjudgmental. Restart with gentle attention to the breath whenever you detect the mind becoming preoccupied with ideas or feelings. As you get more accustomed to the method, progressively extend the duration of this practice. Continue it for a predetermined amount of time.

The Choiceless Awareness practice is an additional guided exercise. Close your eyes and settle into a comfortable sitting position to start. Inhale deeply many times to bring yourself to the present. Whatever comes up, let your awareness be open and responsive to it. Instead of concentrating on anything, notice how ideas, feelings, and sensations come and go. Remain open-minded and curious at all times, avoiding getting sucked into any one event. When you see your mind narrowing in on a particular thing or idea, gently bring your awareness back to the larger realm of experience. Keep doing this for a predetermined amount of time to help you become inclusive and non-discriminatory in your awareness.

When practicing advanced loving-kindness meditation, sit comfortably and shut your eyes. Inhale deeply many times to bring yourself to the present. To begin, focus on loving and caring for yourself and say affirmations to yourself like "May I be happy, may I be healthy, may I be safe." As soon as you experience loving-kindness for yourself, progressively expand this awareness to include loved ones, friends, and ultimately all beings—including those you disagree with or find challenging to deal with. While you are extending loving-kindness to each group, repeat to yourself things like "May you be happy, may you be healthy, may you be safe." Letting go of any aversion or judgment, allow yourself to experience the warmth and compassion in your heart. For a predetermined amount of time, keep up this exercise to develop empathy and unconditional love for all living things.

A guided activity can be used to practice emotion mindfulness. Close your eyes and settle into a comfortable sitting position to start. Inhale deeply many times to bring yourself to the present. Focus on your emotional condition at that moment, taking note of any feelings that come up. Permit yourself to feel it without attempting to control or repress the feeling. Examine the emotion's underlying sources and circumstances while you watch it. Take note of external events, bodily sensations, or ideas influencing the feeling. Recognize that the emotion is fleeting and that it will pass eventually. Bring your focus back to the present and observe the emotion with curiosity and composure if you see any reaction patterns or tendencies. After a predetermined amount of time, keep up this activity to increase your emotional intelligence and resilience.

Additionally, advanced body scan techniques can be supervised. Close your eyes and settle into a comfortable sitting or sleeping position. Inhale deeply many times to bring yourself to the present. Focus on your feet and notice any feelings or energetic patterns there. As you gradually advance up the body, pay close attention to every component, including the arms, legs, torso, and head. Take note of any tense or relaxed spots and any nudges. Let your awareness become granular and precise as you investigate the spectrum of physical sensations. If you perceive any tension or discomfort, bring a sense of calm awareness and acceptance to the area, and then let it soften and dissipate. Maintain this routine for a predetermined time to foster general well-being and a closer relationship with your body.

One way to practice open Monitoring is via a guided exercise. Close your eyes and settle into a comfortable sitting position to start. Inhale deeply many times to bring yourself to the present. Let your awareness be encompassing and comprehensive without concentrating on one thing in particular. Pay attention to how ideas, feelings, and physical sensations come and go. Remain open-minded and curious at all times, avoiding getting sucked into any one event. When you see your mind narrowing in on a particular thing or idea, gently bring your awareness back to the larger realm of experience. Keep up this activity for a predetermined time while keeping your awareness open and responsive.

Investigating more complex mindfulness practices entails developing and broadening mindfulness beyond simple activities. Practitioners can create a more profound and complex experience of mindfulness through advanced techniques like Insight Meditation, voiceless awareness, Sustained Attention, advanced loving-kindness meditation, mindfulness of emotions, advanced body scan techniques, Open Monitoring, and Contemplative Inquiry. Advanced mindfulness activities that are guided can assist people in developing a more thorough practice and exploring various methods in a safe and encouraging environment. Through more advanced mindfulness techniques, people can experience a more profound and life-changing state of awareness by gaining more clarity, composure, and freedom from mental anguish.

The Journey Ahead

The road ahead of you on your mindful journey is full of chances to improve your practice and enhance your life. Being cautious is a continuous process of self-awareness and development rather than a destination. It is a dedication to living in the now, developing consciousness and raising your level of compassion toward both the outside world and one. In the trip ahead, you will learn to incorporate mindfulness more fully into your everyday life, investigate more sophisticated techniques, and use various tools and resources to assist you in maintaining your practice. The subsequent phases in your mindful journey will be discussed in this section, along with the advantages of ongoing training, sophisticated methods, and resources to aid your development.

Make mindfulness a priority in your life to carry on your mindful journey. This is incorporating mindfulness into your regular tasks and routines so that it develops into a habit that is consistent and natural. For instance, you can incorporate mindfulness into your connection with food by practicing mindful eating. A greater appreciation for the sustenance that food offers can be attained by focusing on your food's flavor, texture, and aroma and enjoying every bite. Consider incorporating mindful walking into your regular practice similarly. Strolling may help you stay present and connected to your body and environment, whether in the city, outdoors, or just around your house. Paying conscious attention to the sensations of walking can support this.

You might experiment with more sophisticated methods as you develop your mindfulness practice. These methods can broaden your awareness and improve your comprehension of the mind. Vipassana, also known as insight meditation, is one such advanced technique. Observing all occurrences' transience, dissatisfaction, and selflessness is critical to insight meditation. You can get significant insights into the nature of reality by practicing a deep awareness of the emerging and passing away of ideas, emotions, and sensory sensations. This practice can result in increased mental clarity, composure, and freedom from mental anguish.

A further sophisticated method is Choiceless Awareness. During this exercise, you don't focus on any one particular thing; instead, you stay open and aware of whatever comes into your field of awareness. By promoting an inclusive and non-discriminatory approach to mindfulness, Choiceless Awareness enables you to cultivate a more expansive awareness. By assisting you in escaping routine thought and behavior patterns, this technique can help you develop a more profound sense of openness and presence.

Mindfulness practice can benefit from various tools, resources, and advanced techniques. For many practitioners, mindfulness applications are a well-liked and easily accessible resource. You may stay consistent with your practice by using apps like Headspace, Calm, and Insight Timer, which offer guided meditations, mindfulness classes, and reminders. These apps can help you integrate mindfulness more easily into your everyday life by offering structure and direction. They also provide a range of meditations for various objectives, including regulating emotions, enhancing sleep, and reducing stress.

Reading books about mindfulness can also be a great way to improve your knowledge and skills. Well-known books about mindfulness include "The Miracle of Mindfulness" by Thich Nhat Hanh, "Wherever You Go, There You Are" by Jon Kabat-Zinn, and "The Power of Now" by Eckhart Tolle. These classic works also provide insightful analysis and helpful advice. These works can broaden your understanding, inspire you, and present fresh angles on mindfulness practice. To further assist you on your path, many modern books also address particular facets of mindfulness, such as "The Mindful Path to Self-Compassion" by Christopher Germer and "Radical Acceptance" by Tara Brach.

Taking part in mindfulness retreats is another effective way to advance your practice. Retreats provide a concentrated, intensive setting for mindfulness practice away from the interruptions of everyday life. They frequently consist of instruction from skilled mindfulness trainers, silent periods, and guided meditations. Retreats allow you to develop your practice further, obtain fresh perspectives, and connect with like-minded people. Attending a residential retreat, whether for a weekend or longer, is a life-changing and revitalizing experience.

Communities and groups focused on mindfulness can also provide beneficial connections and support. By joining a community or organization dedicated to mindfulness, you can practice alongside others, exchange experiences, and get support and direction. Numerous communities have regular study groups, workshops, and meditation sessions. You can maintain your commitment to your practice by feeling accountable and like you belong in a mindfulness community. Joining an online community or an in-person organization can provide vital support and connections.

In your continuous mindfulness journey, developing openness and curiosity, in addition to these tools, is crucial. Every moment presents a fresh opportunity for learning and development since mindfulness is a dynamic and ever-evolving practice. Be open to whatever emerges and approach your practice with the mindset of a novice, letting go of expectations. Maintaining an attitude of openness and curiosity will help you stay motivated and involved, enabling your practice to keep developing and getting deeper.

It's crucial to practice self-compassion as you proceed on your mindful journey. Being cautious is about being present and compassionate with yourself every moment, not about reaching perfection or solving problems. Recognize that mindfulness is a lifetime journey and be gentle to yourself when difficulties arise. Your practice will feel intense at times and tough at other times. Accept and show compassion for both, understanding that every moment is a chance for development and education.

Relationship mindfulness is another crucial component of your continuous practice. You may improve communication, build stronger relationships, and cultivate empathy and compassion by paying attention to how you engage with others. Engage in active listening, give others your attention, and answer politely and kindly.

By practicing mindfulness in your relationships, you may foster a more loving and caring atmosphere for yourself and others.

It might also be advantageous to apply mindfulness in your professional life. By improving attention, creativity, and resilience, mindfulness can support you in overcoming the difficulties and expectations of the workplace. To keep focused and grounded throughout the day, engage in mindful breathing exercises or take brief mindfulness breaks. Pay attention to what you do and the people you interact with to be wholly present and involved in your work. Incorporating mindfulness into your work life may increase productivity and well-being while fostering a more harmonious and satisfying work environment.

It's crucial to remember that mindfulness is not just about formal meditation practice as you proceed on your mindful path. Being cautious is a way you practice in every area of your life. Cultivate attention when performing routine tasks like driving, cleaning, or cooking. Pay close attention to your movements, feelings, and environment. You may develop a stronger sense of presence and connection by incorporating mindfulness into every aspect.

In summary, as you proceed on your mindful journey, you will encounter several chances to enhance your practice and improve your quality of life. You can support your continued practice by incorporating mindfulness into your everyday routines, investigating more complex techniques, and using various tools and resources. Communities, retreats, publications, and applications that promote mindfulness can offer insightful direction, motivation, and a sense of community. You can further improve your journey by developing self-compassion, openness, and curiosity and incorporating mindfulness into your relationships and work life. Recall that practicing mindfulness is a lifetime endeavor and that there are always opportunities for development and education. By carrying on with your mindful path, you can develop more awareness, presence, and well-being, as well as a more meaningful and happy existence.

CONCLUSION

As we wrap up our journey with "The Mindful Journey: A Beginner's Guide: Discovering Peace and Clarity in Everyday Life," take a moment to reflect on the path you've traveled and the changes you've initiated. Remember, mindfulness is not a one-time event but a lifelong journey of personal growth and exploration. Every moment is an opportunity to sharpen your awareness, leading to a more peaceful and clear life.

Throughout this book, you've delved into the basics of mindfulness, learned how to integrate it into your daily life, and discovered solutions to common challenges. You've also explored more advanced techniques and how mindfulness can enhance your relationships and overall well-being. Your journey has equipped you with a wealth of knowledge and understanding.

Recall that practicing mindfulness involves embracing each moment as it arises and staying in the present without passing judgment. It is a mild yet effective tool that enables you to handle the highs and lows of life with perseverance and grace. Be kind to yourself as you proceed on your mindful journey. Even though progress is sluggish, each step is a stride toward a calmer, more focused life.

Remember the values and techniques you have acquired. Allow them to lead the way as you proceed, keeping you centered and in the here and now. You are only beginning your mindful journey, and with each conscious breath you take, you are learning to access the deep calm and clarity that are already inside you.

Thank you for buying and reading/ listening to our book. If you found this book useful/ helpful please take a few minutes and leave a review on the platform where you purchased our book. Your feedback matters greatly to us.